DATE DUE

Composers of North America

Series Editors: Sam Dennison, William C. Loring, Margery Lowens, Ezra Schabas

FRANCES McCOLLIN:

Her Life and Music

by
Annette Maria DiMedio

Composers of North America, No. 7

The Scarecrow Press, Inc.
Metuchen, N.J., & London
1990

Frontispiece: Frances McCollin. Photo by Blackstone Studios, New York.

The author gratefully acknowledges all those who granted permission to reprint musical examples. Specific credits appear on pages xii-xiii or with musical examples.

British Library Cataloguing-in-Publication data available

Library of Congress Cataloging-in-Publication Data

DiMedio, Annette Maria, 1958-
    Frances McCollin : her life and music / by Annette Maria DiMedio.
        p.   cm. -- (Composers of North America ; no. 7)
    Includes bibliographical references and index.
    ISBN 0-8108-2289-X
    1. McCollin, Frances, 1892-1960. 2. Composers--Pennsylvania--
Philadelphia--Biography. 3. Blind musicians--Pennsylvania--
Philadelphia--Biography. I. Title. II. Series.
ML410.M452D5   1990
780'.92--dc20
[B]   90-44831

TO CLEMENT C. PETRILLO (1914-1982)

Who has shared with me the power of expression
through music and has shown me through his own example
that with devotion, discipline, and drive,
nothing is impossible.

In the male-dominated world of American music during the first half of the twentieth century, Frances McCollin's life and achievements are nothing short of amazing. An inflammation of the eyes, suffered from her birth in 1892, caused total blindness by age five. Despite this and the disadvantage of being female, she developed a fully successful career as a composer, with 19 national awards, hundreds of performances, and publication of 93 of her 333 compositions. In addition she was active in virtually every aspect of the music world of her time. She conducted, taught, hosted her own radio program, and toiled endlessly in behalf of her fellow American composers.

Outstanding as Frances McCollin's accomplishments were, this study of her life and works represents the first recognition of her many contributions. It is through books such as this that we can fully appreciate this incredible woman's career and ensure her the honored place in America's musical history that is her due.

Dr. Annette DiMedio deserves a full measure of credit for the enormous obstacles she had to contend with to bring this study to its successful completion. Hers was the last dissertation on American composers that was allowed under Bryn Mawr's now defunct graduate music program. Thus Dr. DiMedio had to face the problems of completing her project during the dismantling of the academic support system along with the difficulties encountered in the research itself. It is my privilege to share the forefront with those who state that she has done honor to herself as well as to her subject.

Sam Dennison
Wichita Falls, Texas

As a concert pianist and teacher I have developed an interest in reviving the works of American women composers whose works have not received due attention. I was introduced to the works of the blind Philadelphia-born composer Frances McCollin by Sam Dennison, curator of the Edwin A. Fleisher Music Collection at the Free Library of Philadelphia. The music department of the library offered me the challenge of cataloguing her works from which a life and works study evolved. But not until I opened the first folder of letters did I know that I would take the challenge. The first letter was from conductor Fabien Sevitzky who praised Frances McCollin's works and predicted that some day someone would do a study on her. The letter was dated October 29, 1959, exactly twenty years prior to the day I was reading it. That was only the first of a series of coincidences. She had conducted at Swarthmore College, where I had been an undergraduate. Her sister, Katherine McCollin Arnett, had gone to Bryn Mawr, and her cousin had taught there. When I inquired how I could get in touch with Frances' sister, I was told she resided with her husband at Kendal at Longwood, a retirement center at which I had performed several concerts. Therefore, I indirectly knew Mrs. Arnett. As I began my research, other coincidences began to surface and I felt a close kinship to this woman. Her family was involved with the founding of the Philadelphia Orchestra, with which I had performed as soloist several times. I found that many orchestra members remembered Frances McCollin. In fact it was Mason Jones, French-horn player in the orchestra, who bought her home on 2128 Delancey Place. On February 17, 1980, I was given the opportunity to present one of the Philadelphia Orchestra "talks" before a Friday afternoon concert, as Frances McCollin had done on a regular basis from 1924-1944. I also performed and directed Frances McCollin's music under the auspices of the Musical Fund Society, of which her father was past president.

The great bulk of the documentation of Frances' life and work--scrapbooks, musical scores, correspondence--was transcribed and compiled by other persons, usually friends and members of the family. Even her autobiography was dictated to family members and not written in Frances' own hand. Therefore, the researcher who seeks to know Frances through a perusal of these documents is frustrated in the attempt, since none of the material bears the seal of Frances McCollin. There are no samples of handwriting, no personal notes, diaries, none of the personal memorabilia that surrounds the lives of many composers. One is always left with the feeling of being able to know Frances only from indirect or second-hand sources. This problem could not be overcome by seeking personal interviews with her mother, father, aunt, and close friends, as they were dead when I began my study. Fortunately, Frances' sister, Katherine Arnett, her husband, and children were extremely helpful.

As for the scores, even though they were all in the music department of the library, they had not been organized into a usable collection. Therefore, I chose to catalogue by genre and developed my own system. The information for the compilation of the list of her performances came from well-documented scrapbooks kept by her mother, aunt, and sisters. There were no references in the family collections to performances of her works after her death in 1960. Inquiries to numerous churches and musical organizations helped to fill the gap between 1960 and the present.

The study is divided into three chapters. The first, "The Making of a Blind Composer," deals with Frances McCollin's life and her interrelationships with family, friends, and colleagues. It discusses her acquisition of musical skills, her musical awards, and musical experiences. The second chapter, "The Musical Style of Frances McCollin," elaborates on general characteristics associated with her work on different genres. A section of this chapter outlines certain aspects of Frances' life that are reflected in her music, such as blindness, religion, and pacifism. Chapter 3, "Influences on Frances McCollin's Music," includes the circumstances that contributed to the public reception of her music. Chapter 4 consists of a brief epilogue. Chapter 5 is a listing of McCollin's printed and manuscript scores, all housed in the Free Library of Philadelphia (partly in the Music Department and partly in the Fleisher Collection). Incipits of all the works are included for identification of the works catalogued. The appendices include lists of live performances, awards, and locations of her lectures.

Frances McCollin is an "unsung heroine" who used her musical talent to express a love of God and humanity despite her blindness. She made a positive contribution to society by immortalizing herself through her music and sharing it with others during her lifetime. Probably because of her blindness, she learned how to be dependent upon other people and she enhanced her life and career by building contacts and alliances with others. These alliances encouraged her to compose both secular and sacred music.

My purpose is to reintroduce Frances McCollin in a formal study and make her a "now-sung heroine" by reviving an interest in her musical compositions. To know Frances is to know the people who surrounded her and the circumstances of being a blind woman musician during changing times in Philadelphia. To know her music is to understand Frances McCollin's life from day to day in a world of darkness lighted by her belief in serving God and humanity.

Annette Maria DiMedio
University of the Arts
Philadelphia

Many people helped make this project a reality. I am humbly indebted to them all. It is impossible to enumerate everyone's contribution in detail or mention everyone by name. When I offer a general acknowledgment, I hope that each will recognize his/her part.

Dr. Clement Petrillo, late dean of the Philadelphia College of the Performing Arts and my piano teacher for 18 years, was my chief source of musical inspiration throughout my life and encouraged me to do musical research. The book is dedicated to him.

Frances McCollin's family has been very generous by donating all the manuscripts, printed scores, and memorabilia to the Free Library of Philadelphia. They have also been accommodating with my questions, visits, and interviews. Among these family members, most sincere thanks are extended to the late Dr. and Mrs. John Arnett and to their children, Dr. Edward M. Arnett and Mrs. Alice Arnett Andrews. Dr. Edward Arnett also kindly granted permission to reprint from Frances McCollin's composition "Dear Lord and Father." Sewell Hodge at Kendal at Longwood acted as a liaison between the Arnetts and myself; his help is much appreciated. Other relatives consulted included Mr. and Mrs. Richard Foster and Mrs. Betty Stonorov to whom I am also grateful.

Many other people were eager to share their memories of Frances McCollin and I greatly appreciated the interviews granted me by Jeanne Behrend, W.B. Willard Comstock, Leslie Marles, and Betty Boone. Others, such as Otto Albrecht, Alexander McCurdy, Orlando Cole, Bruce Montgomery, Arthur Cohn, Peter LaManna, and members of the Philadelphia Orchestra, had tidbits of information to share and I thank them for making Frances McCollin come alive as a human being.

People from various institutions took an interest in my project. It was Sam Dennison, curator of the Edwin Fleisher Collection, who first introduced me to Frances McCollin's music, and I thank him for giving me a place to work with the materials in the Fleisher Collection and for advising me on the library's cataloguing procedures. Frederick Kent, head of the Music Department at the Free Library, was also very helpful, especially since he had done a preliminary card catalogue of McCollin scores and memorabilia given to the library. Staff members of both the Fleisher and Music Department were also very supportive of my research. Special thanks go to the members of the Musical Fund Society, especially William Kelley and Boyd Barnard, for hosting and funding the program of Frances McCollin's works on May 17, 1981, at the First Presbyterian Church in Philadelphia.

I am grateful for the cooperation of the Pennsylvania Institute for the Instruction of the Blind as well as the local churches supplying information on performances of Frances McCollin's works throughout the years. It is my hope that some of her works will again be performed in these churches, now that they are accessible at the Free Library.

People who have personally influenced my musical education have had an important bearing on this project. My thanks go to the faculty of the Swarthmore College Music Department, Temple University School of Music faculty, in particular Dr. Eve Meyer and Dr. Sterling Murray who interested me in American music studies, and Bryn Mawr College music faculty, Mr. Robert Goodale and Dr. Carl Schmidt. Special thanks go to my adviser, Dr. Isabelle Cazeaux, for being my mentor during my graduate studies and this project. Members of the library staff, faculty, and administration of the Philadelphia College of the Performing Arts have been supportive and helpful. Bryn Mawr College alumni have been an asset to my study, especially Dr. Martha Schleifer, whose doctoral work concerned William Gilchrist, Frances McCollin's teacher.

I would like to mention those friends who acted as readers and encouraged the project forward such as Dr. William Biddle, Dr. Roy Clouser, Father Joseph Grailey, Dinah Gonzales-Braile, Louis Lombardo, and Daren Hagen. I cannot omit mention of my spiritual network of friends, especially Brother Ronald Farinella, Father Martin Shartz, and Brother Joseph Corrado from the St. Francis Friary. My friends are very special to me and I thank them for being a part of my life and work.

I have been blessed with a family that matched moral with practical support on this project. My parents have always been an integral part of my education, financing my endeavors as well as giving me the opportunity to choose a career in music. Along with general support from my aunts and uncles as well as my Grandmother Verdi, my sister Regina as performer and conductor of Frances McCollin's works in concert with me, my youngest sister Lisa as my general assistant, and my brother, Mark, and Mom as proofreaders--all made this project a reality. I am proud, lucky, and thankful to have such a wonderful, loving family as another part of my support system.

HAROLD FLAMMER, INC.

"In the Clock Shop at Three." Copyright 1940, Harold Flammer, Inc.; Delaware Water Gap, PA 19327. All Rights reserved. Used with permission.

THEODORE PRESSER CO.

"Berceuse," ©1918; "Christmas Lullaby," © 1937, 1938; "Come Hither Ye Faithful," © 1927; "God So Loved the World," © 1914; "The Holy Birth," ©1930; "How Living Are the Dead," © 1944; "In Fairyland--Suite for Violin," © 1928; "Jubilate Deo," ©1916; "My Peace I Leave with You," © 1926; "A New Commandment Give I unto You," © 1916; "The Nights o' Spring," ©1919; "O Lamb of God," © 1907; "Pack Clouds Away," ©1942; "Resurrection," © 1927; "Rondo," ©1920; "A Roundelay," © 1925; "Shouting Sun," © 1934; "The Singing Leaves," © 1918; "Sleep Holy Babe," ©1930; "The Sleeping Beauty," © 1917; "A Song of Spring," © 1934; "Spring in Heaven," © 1931; "Thou Art Like unto a Flower," © 1910; "The Way of the Cross," © 1928; "What Care I?" ©1923. Copyright © by Oliver Ditson Company and Theodore Presser Company. Copyrights used by permission of the publisher.

Frances McCollin, the first-born child of Edward Garrett McCollin and Alice Graham Lanigan McCollin, came into the world on October 24, 1892, at 927 Clinton Street, Philadelphia. According to the Evening Bulletin, the weather was fair that Monday, the stock market opened with a boom, and the former First Lady, Mrs. Harrison, was "passing into Death's shadows."[1] In the Philadelphia Inquirer World of Women column for that same day, Dorothy Maddox's headline read: "Opportunities [for women] for Self Culture and Advancement Each Day Grow More Numerous," almost sounding like a message from a fortune cookie meant for the birthday girl, Frances McCollin.[2]

Frances came by her love of music quite naturally, perhaps even inevitably, as her family was very active in the Philadelphia musical scene. As an undergraduate at the University of Pennsylvania, Edward McCollin studied musical composition with Dr. Hugh Clark, receiving a certificate for work in this field. In 1880, he earned his law degree at the University of Pennsylvania followed by a Master of Arts in 1881. Whereas law was his profession, he was an amateur organist and violinist who spent his leisure performing in chamber groups and composing. He wrote a number of songs and choral pieces for male, female, and mixed voices, sacred and secular, which were published by Schirmer, Ditson, and others. Among these are two popular University of Pennsylvania songs, "Ben Franklin" and "Pennsylvania Girl."[3]

However, his interest in music was not limited to composition and performance. He also contributed substantially to the development of musical institutions. Edward McCollin was one of the founders of the Philadelphia Orchestra in 1900 and a member of its Board of Directors from 1900 to 1908.[4] He also served as vice-president of the Musical Fund Society from 1901 to 1910 and as president until his death in 1923.[5] He developed musical societies in Philadelphia, such as the University of Pennsylvania Glee Club, in 1922, and the Manuscript Society of Philadelphia.[6] Besides all this, Edward McCollin was one of the earliest members of the Orpheus Club, served as its president at one point, and was its chief baritone soloist.[7] From all his activities it is apparent Edward McCollin spent at least as much time with his avocation, music, as he did with law. He died of Parkinson's disease on November 24, 1923, at the age of 65 when Frances was 31 years old. He had been the major figure in his blind daughter's life, introducing her to music, teaching her the fundamentals of composition, and helping her experience the musical scene in Philadelphia. His death left Frances dependent upon her mother for the remainder of her life.

Alice Graham Lanigan McCollin's background was more literary than musical. Her father was the Irish-Canadian poet George T. Lanigan and her mother worked for Edward Bok's publications as editor until 1903.[8] Later Alice followed in her mother's footsteps, working as associate food editor of Ladies' Home Journal until her marriage to Edward Garrett McCollin in Philadelphia on October 28, 1891. As for her contributions to the musical world, Alice McCollin helped organize the first Women's Committee of the Philadelphia Orchestra in 1904 and acted as corresponding secretary. She was also president of the Women's Committee of the Philadelphia Chamber String Sinfonietta under Fabien Sevitzky. Alice Graham McCollin died on October 20, 1958, at the age of 90.[9] Her daughter Frances died the following year. If Edward McCollin taught Frances the technical fundamentals of music, Alice McCollin's contribution to Frances' musical career lay more in the promotional area. Mrs. McCollin's participation in numerous musical societies and organizations gave her the opportunity and the influence to bring her daughter's music to the attention of the Philadelphia public.

The musical interest of Katherine McCollin, Frances' younger sister by sixteen months, was primarily vocal. Several times it was Katherine (nicknamed "Kitty" by Frances) who introduced Frances' songs by performing them in public. She also composed vocal works under the pen name "Frank Shepherdson."[10] She sang in a number of choral groups, one of which became the setting of her romance with Dr. John Arnett, a physician whom she later married. She graduated from Bryn Mawr College in 1915. Dr. Arnett was a graduate of the University of Pennsylvania and a member of the prominent Philadelphia family of Arnetts. His mother, a member of the Women's Committee of the Philadelphia Orchestra, along with Alice McCollin, also helped to found another auxiliary, the Rittenhouse Square Women's Committee for the Philadelphia Orchestra. After their mother's death, Kitty took Frances into her own home at 6200 Ardleigh Avenue. Here, Frances received excellent medical care from Dr. Arnett through the last year of her life.

Dr. and Mrs. Arnett resided at Kendal at Longwood until their recent deaths. Kitty's role was that of the supportive sister who recognized Frances' talent as a musician, promoting her work during her lifetime and even after her death. Kitty also saw herself as the protector of her older sister and saw to her sister's needs, particularly after the death of their mother.

The fact that Frances became totally blind at the age of five was the major factor in shaping her personality and caused a lifelong dependency upon members of her family.[11] Although Frances adapted well to her handicap, she was always aware of her blindness, although not morbidly obsessed by it. In her autobiography, she comments on her blindness in this way: "Blindness is of course a handicap but in my opinion as one blinded from childhood it is not an affliction. A blind child can be a happy child, and it would have been the same in my childhood, even if there had not been money for pleasures, for love was the cornerstone of the whole family."[12]

She even wrote a witty catalogue of the various reactions people display upon meeting a blind person, drawn from her experience in walks around Rittenhouse Square.[13]

Type A-1 The Dresden China or the Invalid Type
In the house--"Sit here dear. Here's your fork and your coffee is at the right, right here. Oh, there's the phone, don't move till I come back. Is the room too warm for you dear?" Etc.
Outside--in the street--"Now down a step dear, down a step, now hurry there's a truck coming, now up, are you alright dear?"

Type A-2 The Deaf Type
In the house--at meals--"Will she have light or dark meat? Shall I give her some gravy? Does she prefer vanilla or strawberry?" Etc.
Shopping--"Does she want this? Does she want two or one? Shall I hand that to her myself? Bring her this way, up these stairs." Etc.

Type B-1 Old Ladies with False Teeth and Not Much Sense of Humor
"Oh you're so wonderful. Ts.ts.ts. With that terrible affliction my dear child. You know, I never appreciated my two good eyes, til I knew you. You make us appreciate our blessings, dear, you do indeed. You know there are compensations and that is good."

Type B-2 Very Boring
"Oh my but you're cheerful! You know if I were that, I'd be crying all day and you keep me laughing. It's just grand, you can be so cheerful."

Type B-3A This Type Never Speaks
They come up and look at you and crane their necks to be sure you're really blind. They walk off with an expression of triumph as if they'd seen a zoo animal.

Type B-3B Walks Off with an Expression
--"Yes, poor girl, she is."

Type C-1 This Is the Worst of All
"Who am I, my dear, who am I? Don't tell her, Mrs. Soobs, don't tell her." "I'll guess Mrs. Smith." "Try again, dear." Then they mention an important blind

person--"So and so always knew my handclasp." (Mrs. Soobs aside--"Mrs. Jones.")
"Mrs. Jones." "That's right, dear, I knew you'd get it."

Although Frances did not believe her handicap diminished her worth as a human being, she did express concern that colleagues might overpraise her work out of pity instead of on its artistic merits. Winning national awards by using pen names such as Hancock, Pastor, or Atticus helped to boost her confidence that she was being judged on a competitive basis with fellow composers.[14]

As a result of her handicap, Frances received more care and attention from all the members of her extended family than a normal child would have.[15] Her father personally attended to her musical education; her godmother, Aunt Edith, read literary masterpieces to her and even learned braille to help Frances communicate. Frances' mother played hymns for her; and her niece and nephews took her for walks in Rittenhouse Square.[16] This family-oriented situation both helped and hindered Frances' development. On the one hand, she received a more structured and thorough education than might have been the case if she had been a sighted child. Her musical gifts were discovered, encouraged, and cultivated more intensively than might have occurred otherwise. This state of material dependency on others extended into her adulthood.

She relied on others to collect and record her life's works. Her mother, godmother Aunt Edith, and her sister Katherine, kept meticulous account of Frances' musical achievements, correspondence with publishers and friends, as well as royalty statements, awards, and files. Also the family collected and donated both the published scores and manuscripts to the Fleisher Collection and Music Department of the Free Library.[17]

Others transcribed her compositions on paper. Her earliest transcriber was her father (up until 1908).[18] Other transcribers included Leslie Marles and Roma Angel, both Philadelphia musicians, both handicapped.[19] Leslie Marles recalled his experience as her transcriber: "When she would compose she would do dictation with the piano or out of her head. She would go through line by line in her mind before sitting down at the piano so I could check my dictation. We rarely went back for corrections but sometimes I would catch an error and she would have to fix it."[20]

At various times many others helped with transcribing: Dr. Timmings, organist and choirmaster; Vincent Persichetti, composer, pianist, and representative of Elkan Vogel; Jeanne Behrend, composer and pianist; and Fabien Sevitzky, double bass player of the Philadelphia Orchestra and conductor. Still others helped her with revisions: Horatio Parker (Yale University Department of Music), George Chadwick (then dean of New England Conservatory), Lucien Caillet, Roger Sessions, Helen Leavitt (from Ginn Company), Gena Branscombe, Dr. Gilchrist, and H. Alexander Matthews, her composition teacher.[21]

Financially she was dependent on her father's savings and members of the family like Aunt Edith, her sister Kitty, and Dr. John Arnett. Frances did make money on her own from teaching, lecturing, and royalties, but none of those made her totally financially independent.[22]

All these circumstances inevitably led to a permanent state of dependency that prevented Frances from maturing and kept her in many respects a child for the rest of her life. She never developed emotionally or socially to the point of being able to have intimate interpersonal relationships. Outside of her family, she had no intimate friendships, no suitors, and never married. She seemed unable to relate to people on an adult level except in the teacher-student relationship. Even as an older woman, she would engage in children's games.

Having considered the social, intellectual, and artistic circumstances from which Frances McCollin came, we can now examine the technical aspects of her musical education. It was her father who first discovered her musical abilities. He patiently but methodically nurtured them by keeping copious notes on her progress as early as 1894, when she was only two years of age.[23] In her autobiography, Frances claimed that musical talent was "in the genes" on her father's side with Grandmother McCollin, her father's first teacher. Grandmother Lanigan could not carry a tune and when she did sing, Frances invariably cried. In an essay about her early love of music, she writes:

From the time I was a baby, the world of sound was everything to me. My family
lost no opportunity in encouraging their rather difficult baby daughter; buying me
a Regina Music Box and playing the piano for me at every available moment. Anything
that could be listened to was my delight; church bells, canary birds, hand organs;
everything from Beethoven to "Paradise Alley." From the time I could walk, I loved
to go and touch the piano.[24]

Before she was a year old, Frances showed that she recognized three tunes to which she
clapped her hands in time: "Oh yes I am a Dutchman," "Polly put the kettle on," and "There
was a little woman as I've heard tell." At 14 months, her father bought her several books of
nursery songs. She learned ten tunes the first week, recognizing the tunes by certain words
like "tea," for "Polly put the kettle on" or "buns," for "Hot cross buns."[25] At fourteen and
a half months old, she put three notes together in this tune:

which she could sing in the keys of E, D, or C associating them with her "Papa." When he
came home at night or into the room she would call "Papa" and sing the notes until he replied.
Although Frances showed unusual talent at such a young age, it wasn't until the age of five
that she received instruction in the rudiments of the art.

Immediately after beginning instruction, Frances could distinguish intervals and hear the
difference between a melody written in a major key and one written in a minor key. In his
memoirs her father wrote repeatedly, "She required no further instruction but my once telling
her."[26] In October of the same year, Edward McCollin taught her the notes on the piano. Within three weeks with sessions lasting only ten minutes on any one day and usually no more than
twice a week, she not only knew the keyboard, both black and white keys (she could still distinguish color at this point), but she could recognize major and minor scales.[27]

Further musical education included hearing rehearsals of the Thunder Orchestra, made
up of members of the then defunct Philadelphia Germania Orchestra.[28] One day on the way
home from a rehearsal at the Musical Fund Hall in Philadelphia, Frances and her mother were
in the station waiting for the train. Frances heard a loud noise and remarked in a piercing
voice, "Mother, what a funny horn." Mother whispered into her ear, "It wasn't a horn dear,
it was a man blowing his nose." Frances said aloud, "But it was in D-flat."[29]

Her study was interrupted by a serious illness that lasted about three weeks. For a brief
period she lost her interest in music, but by the end of November (1897) she was eager to continue her lessons. Her father showed her how to play the scale of C Major, calling it a "tune."
She had heard him do "tunes" like this on his viola. He introduced her to minor scales of various forms at the same time. The raised keys (black keys) were easier for her to distinguish
with her fingers; therefore, her favorite keys were those beginning on raised notes, which
as a rule are technically more difficult for people to play. She also learned to play major and
minor tonic triads, dominant seventh chords, and was able to make proper resolutions to the
tonic.

By six years of age she advanced to finger exercises at the keyboard and was able to
identify augmented sixth and seventh chords and their resolutions.[30] She spent a great part
of her day at the piano trying experiments in different keys with the material which she had
been given from time to time. She regarded this as a matter of play and kept going back to
it in between playing with Kitty, her sister, and her dolls. She played with the harmonies.
She talked to them as if they were animate objects. When she made mistakes with her fingering
she'd call herself or the notes "naughty" or said "goodbye" to different notes and harmonies.
She used the proper phrasing and correct rhythms when she played symphony melodies on the
piano. Her sense of absolute pitch had developed to the extent that she could spell consonant
or dissonant chords with six of seven notes.[31] The comprehension she demonstrated of different scales and chords at the early age of six indicated that she had not only a natural gift
of absolute pitch, but also musical intelligence. Reflecting on this newfound skill Frances
wrote:

> This opened a new door for me. I suddenly learned that hand organs were usually in
> D; that Beethoven's Fifth Symphony was in A-Flat [second movement] and my beloved
> Regina Music Box was in B-Flat with excursions into its related keys. My other music
> box was in A-flat, with excursions of the same nature. The whistle on the Power House
> was "my beloved A-Flat minor triad whistle." One of the worst nightmares I ever had
> was that my second music box played "Lucia" in B-Flat instead of A-Flat. I wept and
> would not be comforted. [32]

Frances not only associated keys with objects but also with various colors and moods,
thereby demonstrating a synesthetic approach to music. The color green reminded her of E
major, a darker green E-Flat major. The key of F Major which was her favorite key, possibly
because her name began with the letter "F" and her mother's voice was in the key of F, was
associated with the color pink. If a person who reminded her of F major was not feeling so
well, she would say, "Yes, she is feeling rather F-minorish this morning." For a blind person
to think in terms of color seems odd to a sighted person. Frances could still distinguish color
until the age of five, but even if she could not recall her color experiences, it would not be
out of the ordinary to relate to them as a blind person. Helen Keller in her book The World
I Live In makes several allusions to color:

> Thus through an inner law of completeness my thoughts are not to be permitted to
> remain colorless. It strains my mind to separate color and sound from objects. Since
> my education began I have always had things described to me with their colors and
> sounds.... Therefore, I habitually think of things as colored and resonant. The
> unity of the world demands that color be kept in it whether I have cognizance of it
> or not. [33]

At a very young age, Frances began implementing the new skills she was acquiring through
composing small pieces of her own. Frances' earliest composition written at the age of three
was inspired by the neighboring rooster named McLochlin, who, according to Frances, crowed
in the key of E. [34] The rhythm of the train wheels reminded her of a waltz melody in the key
of F which her mother played on the piano. It gave Frances the idea for her Freight Train
Tune in 4/4 time which she sang in her crib. [35] She composed tunes at this time about her
family and her playthings. With her own words she created tunes like "Sister's Hair," and
"The Paper Doll Box." It was easy for Frances since she had such an incredible imagination.
Her creativity developed in both a musical and literary sense. From her experience at Woodside
Park and the Atlantic City merry-go-round, she took the tunes and composed a play. She enjoyed making up games and nonsense songs and enjoyed creating imaginary people with whom
she could talk as she walked in the yard. [36] When she told funny stories, her sense of humor
was evident through her dramatized characters. She also made up her own language, including
special words for things and people she loved. She called her house Soobsville and her mother
Mrs. "Soobs" and "Gaga," and named her nephews "Old Codger" and "Pfuffy." Her braille
typewriter bore the name "Typsy." For things not so nice, like the drenched cat coming into
the house out of a storm, she would use the word "Ewr." [37] These words were also used by
her friends. In the guest book of 2128 Delancey Place, there is a poem "To Frances and Mrs.
Soobs." [38]

Frances' formal education began in the fall of 1899 at the age of seven. For two years
she went to a private school run by her Aunt Edith and a friend. At this school, located two
doors from home, she studied all the subjects the other children took, except spelling, which she
did privately with her aunt. Aunt Edith also introduced her to authors such as Louisa May
Alcott, Robert Louis Stevenson, Rudyard Kipling, and James Whitcomb Riley, whom Frances
would use as sources for texts of her music. Later, Frances would spend intermittent time
at the kindergarten for the blind which had moved from its Philadelphia location to Overbrook
in 1898. Frances never liked it, preferring her aunt's school which she attended regularly.

Frances' formal education was frequently interrupted by absences from school due to ill
health. She was a very nervous child, subject to nasty tantrums and crying spells. At times,
she bit her sister and broke her toys, and tore her sister's favorite pictures. The crying spells
were outlets for depression. [39] When she attended the dress rehearsal of the first concert of
the Philadelphia Orchestra (November 16, 1900) she heard the slow movement of Beethoven's
Fifth Symphony, which made her think of the deaf Beethoven and she burst into tears. [40] These

health problems, which began to manifest themselves during her school years, were to continue throughout her life. In later life she received blood tests and vitamin treatments from Dr. Arnett, with little improvement. Her illness stemmed from irregular sleeping habits, something quite common with blind people.[41] She could only put herself to sleep by remembering what happened one year from a certain day, two years from a certain day, etc.[42] The depression became so severe that in her late twenties Frances even contemplated suicide.[43]

Between the ages of six and twelve (1899-1904), Frances studied piano privately with Miss Small at the Pennsylvania Institute for the Instruction of the Blind, although she did not formally enroll as a day student at the school until 1902.[44] Miss Small's biggest difficulty in teaching Frances was to keep her from playing by ear. Frances liked to sit at the piano and play merry-go-round or hand-organ tunes, and imitate roosters, church bells, and train whistles. But by the spring of 1900, Frances was playing little duets by Diabelli and she began composing pieces reminiscent of Diabelli's studies, using harmonic principles for the first time. Her father copied them down note for note as she played, without offering suggestions of any kind and leaving mistakes uncorrected.[45]

In the spring of 1904 Dr. David Wood, blind organist and Director of Music at the Institute, auditioned Frances and said he would like to have her study with him the following fall. Despite the honor, Frances' attachment to Miss Small made her reluctant to change.[46] Nevertheless, Frances studied piano with Dr. Wood for the next three years and organ for about three months. She recounts her relationship with Dr. Wood in her autobiography:

> Unfortunately I did not get from him what I should have. Though I was musically ready for him at the time, I was too immature in every way. With all my deep love for my music, I was a little girl at first. I remember one time annoying him by asking him if I could give up practicing that day, for it was Kitty's birthday. Of course he said "yes" but he was not at all pleased. And he was quite right. And another thing; I never liked to practice; I would rather play the music I loved; and Mr. Wood was accustomed to ambitious pupils who really liked to work. The third year I was with him was my first year at school with sister. I think emotionally he resented my leaving the Blind School. It had been good enough for him, why not for me?[47]

After studying with Dr. Wood until 1907, Frances studied composition with H. Alexander Matthews and William Gilchrist.[48]

Although music was the focal point of Frances' formal education, she also developed a lively interest in a number of other topics. While at the Institution for the Blind, Frances developed an interest in birds. Her second-grade teacher, Miss Mary Quinn, was a bird lover and encouraged Frances' interest through bird walks and bird study.[49] Frances distinguished different kinds of birds by their calls. In 1903, she composed a piece inspired by woodthrush calls, in 3-part harmony. And in later musical compositions such as Suburban Sketches and Robin Little Robin she makes use of the bird calls she recognized and loved.

In 1907, when Frances was fifteen, the principal of the Pennsylvania Institution for the Blind advised Frances' parents to see if she could be accepted at Miss Wright's (all-girls') school in Bryn Mawr, which her sister Kitty was attending. When Miss Wright heard of the idea, she had Frances come to visit the school for two weeks and take classes. After consultation with her faculty, she informed the McCollins that, although she could not promise that Frances would make progress, she would admit her to the school. Frances recounted the first day in her memoirs:

> So the very thought of going to school with "seeing girls" filled me with joy. October 2, 1907, was a great day. I kept for many years my first school ticket. And when I went to our first basketball game, I begged to be allowed to carry the school flag so that everyone on the train would know that I really went to Miss Wright's school.[50]

By May of that same year, Frances had already composed her first anthem, a very simple setting of the "Agnus Dei." And from 1907 to 1909, she composed several other hymns. Because of her enjoyment of the choir literature she had sung, her first important interest was directed to choral music. When she played the final version of her "Agnus Dei" for her father, he wrote it down. The following Christmas, he surprised her with printed copies. He had sold the music to Presser's Publishing Company. Frances received a five dollar bill as her first royalty. She later recalled spending it:

> I wanted to spend it all for ice cream and candy. But my wise mother persuaded me
> to put it aside and we bought a garnet bracelet. The fact that I wanted to spend it
> in that foolish way is a further proof of how very slowly I was maturing.[51]

The "Agnus Dei" was only the beginning of a multifaceted composing career. During the years Frances pursued her formal education, her spiritual education was enhanced by her exposure to religious services at the Memorial Church of St. Paul in Overbrook.[52]

Her mother and father were two of the founders of the Memorial Church of St. Paul in Overbrook; Frances attended Sunday School at the church until 1905. At the age of eleven, the religious influence began to affect her life. A contralto soloist in St. Paul's Choir, Maude Sproule, requested that Frances sing with the choir.[53] Before church each Sunday, Mr. McCollin rehearsed the hymns with Frances at the piano, playing the alto part by itself, which Frances sang with him. After several repetitions, he then played the other three parts, making Frances sing the alto part on her own. When Mr. McCollin was away in the summer he wrote out by hand the way one would write a tune in braille and mailed it to Frances, expecting her to memorize it and play it for him when he returned.

Frances' understanding of religion grew through her exposure to sacred music. Frances recollects in her own autobiography:

> During Holy Week, 1906, the choir sang "O Day of Penitence" [sic] by Gounod and at
> the rehearsal, I was moved to floods of tears.... The seed had been sown. Was it
> possible that that brave man, who was killed so long ago, cared about me?[54]

Later in life she considered herself "Christian with Episcopalian Sauce." Even though she was brought up in an Episcopal Church, to her, there was only one church in the Body of Christ. In her view all churches were equal.[55]

Her faith and her Quaker ancestry helped mold her attitude of pacifism. She acted upon this philosophy during the World War II era. Frances handed out cards to taxicab drivers telling them to resist going to war. She offered to go to jail for peace, and was even investigated by the FBI for writing letters to servicemen.[56] Her active involvement as a pacifist was demonstrated by her affiliation with the Women's International League for Peace and Freedom, Central Committee for Conscientious Objectors, and The Fellowship of Reconciliation.[57] Some of the titles and literary texts of her musical compositions also exhibit traces of pacifism which will be discussed in the second chapter.

Having considered the early life, education, and musical formation of Frances McCollin, we can now turn our attention to her works and how they were championed by a number of influential figures and institutions.

Over her lifetime, Frances wrote 333 compositions of which 93 were published by Schmidt, Boston Music, C. C. Birchard, Carl Fischer, Presser, Ditson, Schirmer, and others. Her instrumental works include compositions for piano, organ, violin, organ and harp, violoncello and piano, chamber groups, string orchestra, symphony orchestra, and school orchestra. Her vocal works vary from vocal solo and duet, to unison children's songs, to vocal combinations of women's and men's voices, full chorus, a cappella and accompanied. The words are both sacred and secular. Of these, it was her vocal works that gained the most recognition during her lifetime. According to John Tasker Howard in Our American Music, studying with Dr. Gilchrist equipped Frances McCollin with her teacher's uncanny faculty for winning prizes.[58]

Between 1916 and 1947 Frances won 19 national awards and 18 of those were for vocal works. Her vocal works were honored by organizations such as the Manuscript Music Society, Matinee Music Club, National Federation of Music Clubs, Mendelssohn Club, Strawbridge and Clothier Radio Competition, Dayton Westminster Choir, Sigma Alpha Iota, Eurydice Choir, Capital University, Pennsylvania Federation of Music Clubs, and the Harvey Gaul Competition.[59] In

1940-41 she was entered into Who's Who in the East, and in 1951 given the Distinguished Daughters of Pennsylvania Award. The newspapers and musical magazines made public her honors. In an article published by the Philadelphia Public Ledger on March 30, 1918, the headline read: "A New First for Philadelphia and a Girl!"[60] The article was a tribute to the fact that she was the first woman to win the American Guild of Organists' Clemson Prize. The Kimball Prize she won from the Chicago Madrigal Club was also a first by a woman composer. Winning these competitions not only brought honor and attention to Frances during her lifetime, but also presented opportunities for having her pieces performed and published. Private recordings were done by musician friends such as pianist Elisabeth Gittlen, organist Alexander McCurdy, and vocalist Hilda Finley. Public recordings were done by the College of William and Mary and the Morningside College Choir.[61] Also because of the increasing popularity of the area's numerous singing societies, which thirsted for new repertoire, as well as the needs of the local churches for good vocal and organ music to enhance the services, Frances McCollin's works were frequently performed during her lifetime.

Although her instrumental works did not gain the same recognition as her vocal compositions and did not win awards, they were not entirely ignored during Frances' lifetime. Her orchestral compositions were performed by the Philadelphia Orchestra under both Leopold Stokowski and Eugene Ormandy, the Robin Hood Dell Orchestra, the Warsaw (Poland) Philharmonic in Poland, People's Symphony of Boston, the Philadelphia Chamber String Sinfonietta, the Indianapolis Symphony, the Vancouver Symphony Orchestra, and several others. Her chamber works, such as the String Quartet in F and the Sextette in F for Strings, were performed by members of the Philadelphia Orchestra and the Curtis String Quartet.[62] Frequently the compositions were dedicated to the musicians who performed them and in turn compositions by others were dedicated to her.[63] She became acquainted with many famous people of her time such as Marian Anderson, Cecile Chaminade, Mrs. H.H.A. Beach, and Hall Johnson. Many of them dined at her home.[64] She even met and spoke to Igor Stravinsky on January 30, 1925, when the Women's Committee for the Philadelphia Orchestra had a reception for him.

The biggest champion of Frances McCollin's music was Fabien Sevitzky. A White Russian, he had escaped the Soviet Union and come to America in 1918. He played the double bass in the Philadelphia Orchestra from 1923 to 1930. He was the nephew of Koussevitzky but because of the bad relationship between the two of them, he changed his name to Sevitzky. He became a good friend of Frances McCollin and her mother and adopted them as his family. Later he decided to pursue conducting and was appointed conductor of the Philadelphia Chamber String Sinfonietta and the Indianapolis Symphony through the promotional backing of Mrs. McCollin. His wife, Maria Koussevitzky, gave many public performances of Frances' vocal works.

It was Fabien Sevitzky who encouraged many transcriptions of Frances' works. For instance, the composition "A Prayer" was originally composed as an "a cappella chorus" in 1930 and Sevitzky liked it so much that he commissioned Frances through the Philadelphia Chamber String Sinfonietta to do an orchestral transcription, which was completed on March 13, 1933. Sevitzky himself conducted it many times. Frances McCollin's chorale preludes, "All Glory, Laud and Honor" and "Now All the Woods Are Sleeping" were originally for organ. They have been transcribed for string orchestra. Some of the movements of her Suite in F for string sextet were transcribed for string orchestra as part of the Suite for Strings, and the "Adagio" for string orchestra was originally the slow movement of the string quartet written in 1920.[65] Leopold Stokowski was impressed by the talent of Frances McCollin. He performed her works during different Philadelphia Orchestra seasons. In a letter to the editor of the Evening Ledger in 1933, Stokowski said: "Philadelphia can be proud of Frances McCollin, who demonstrates women can be creative as well as men."[66] Stokowski allowed her and no one else to attend the rehearsals of the Philadelphia Orchestra. In return, she was an avid admirer of Stokowski. When he was to resign, she circulated a petition in his support as a great musician and an asset to the Philadelphia music scene and orchestra.[67]

Eugene Ormandy also considered Frances to have a special talent. After a performance of her "Scherzo, Heavenly Children at Play," January 22, 1940, Eugene Ormandy writes: "Your success last week more than proved that I was right when I said the 'Scherzo' is a work of an excellent composer with all the necessary background to become an outstanding composer and one who is constantly growing. The orchestra members felt likewise about your talent."[68]

The newspaper agreed with Ormandy. The Evening Bulletin reviewed the "Scherzo," when it was performed by the Robin Hood Dell Orchestra (under Alexander Smallens), and pronounced it "well-written" and "skillfully scored."[69] Philadelphia Inquirer critic Linton Martin praised the Philadelphia Orchestra's performance of the "Adagio" (under Leopold Stokowski) saying: "The Adagio is a scholarly fine grained work in a sustained mood of reverie and somewhat ecclesiastical in its contemplative character avoiding any hint of ultra modern affections in its smooth harmonic and melodic progressions. It offers nothing to offend the ear or emotions and displays unerring musical sensibility."[70]

The most dramatic newspaper account of one performance done by the Philadelphia Sinfonietta Orchestra of Frances McCollin's work "Scherzo" headlined its article: "Jazz Jolts Effect of Classic Music--Traditions Are Shattered When Hearer Calls Out Demand for Repetition."

> Leaping to his feet before the handclapping had subsided, this ardent individual, a well known organist of the city called to the conductor, "As a member of the audience, I ask that we hear Miss McCollin's work again." There was a flurry of applause, pierced by the words "No! No!" in a piping feminine voice identified as modest Miss McCollin. But Mr. Sevitzky bowed assent and the work was repeated.[71]

The contribution of Frances McCollin and her music was not limited to public performance of her works and recognition by the media. She gave unselfishly of her talents as a teacher interested in the development of young musicians and as a public lecturer on music appreciation.

Frances McCollin lectured on the weekly Philadelphia Orchestra programs, using the piano to demonstrate her points. Linton Martin, music critic of the Philadelphia Inquirer comments on her style:

> Miss McCollin has the felicitous faculty of combining a lively sense of humor with the soundest musical erudition, thoroughly humanizing her presentation of the most conservative classics. So graphic is her manner of delineating the works to be presented that her Music Talks really constitute a performance in miniature. [72]

She gave similar talks in Baltimore, Chicago, Indianapolis, Pittsburgh, and at the Bach Festival in Bethlehem, Pennsylvania, where she staunchly advocated modern composition and continually pleaded for an unbiased attitude toward new music.[73]

For one season she conducted a weekly children's radio program, "I Love Music Club," called the "Aunt Frances Music Hour."[74] Her music also served as background for an educational film presented by the Board of Education in 1949, which was part of the Series of Arts Programs for Philadelphia Schools.

Her teaching career led her to conduct her own compositions in schools. For eleven years, 1922-1933, Ms. McCollin conducted a chorus of girls at the School for the Blind in West Philadelphia. In the 1923-24 season, she led the Girl's Glee Club at Swarthmore College. The group was later called the Swarthmore College Choral Society.[75]

Frances McCollin's health deteriorated during the last 20 years of her life. She suffered several strokes over a period of years and was beset with nervous disorders, insomnia, and other physical problems, according to Dr. John Arnett, her attending physician. Her musical production diminished considerably and few major compositions appeared after 1940, with occasional exceptions such as "It Was a Lover and His Lass" (1951), which won the National Federation of Music Clubs' award in 1951. It is possible that Frances McCollin's poor health at this time affected her rate of musical production.

Another explanation for the few compositional efforts could be that Frances McCollin's interests during her final two decades shifted from composition and performance to musical education and participation in cultural and civic groups. Frances McCollin was very supportive of music clubs both nationally and locally. Being a member of these clubs, Frances helped to promote the works of other women composers. In turn, many of them helped to get her music heard throughout the years. Some of these clubs included ASCAP, the National Federation of

Music Clubs, the Matinee Music Club, the New Century Club, the National Association of American Composers and Conductors, the American Composers Alliance, the American Guild of Organists, and the Philadelphia Art Alliance.[76]

Being a teacher and a member of the growing musical scene in Philadelphia, she actively participated in the further development and promotion of young talent. In an interview, she said she wanted to see American musical talent recognized as the greatest in the world. She also wanted Philadelphia to be acknowledged as the music center of the world, "not as an autocrat but as the servant of music."[77]

Frances McCollin died at 5 P.M. on February 25, 1960, at the University of Pennsylvania Hospital after suffering a third stroke.[78] She was buried at West Laurel Hill Cemetery in Philadelphia. The Memorial Service was held two days later at the Trinity Memorial Chapel, 22nd and Spruce streets, where members of the Philadelphia Orchestra paid their last tribute to her by playing her string quartet.[79]

Her entire life had been devoted to music. Her music was her ministry to God and humanity. As the Public Ledger had put it so well in 1918: "With Frances McCollin, a light shines to the womanhood of America."[80]

NOTES

1. Evening Bulletin, October 24, 1892, p. 7.

2. Philadelphia Inquirer, October 24, 1892, p. 5.

3. Edward Garrett McCollin, "The Record of the Class of 1878" (1899), pp. 104-108. See item 8 in bibliography: memorabilia of Frances McCollin.

4. The other founder of the Philadelphia Orchestra was Dr. Edward Keefer, neighbor of the McCollins and amateur violinist who played chamber music with Mr. McCollin.

5. The Musical Fund Society was founded in 1820 by a group of Philadelphia musicians, composers, authors and professional men who met weekly to play for their own enjoyment. The first concerts were held in Washington Hall, the New Theatre in Chestnut Street and St. Stephen's Church prior to opening of the Musical Fund Hall in 1824. The Musical Fund Society's original purpose was twofold; first, it was a relief source for needy musicians and second, advanced musical taste through instrumental and vocal concerts. It is the oldest American musical organization in continuous existence.

6. The Manuscript Society of Philadelphia was founded by William Gilchrist in 1892 and also conducted by him. The society sponsored concerts of new compositions by local composers given in rooms and halls in Philadelphia. See Martha Furman Schleifer, William Wallace Gilchrist (1846-1916): A Moving Force in the Musical Life of Philadelphia (Metuchen, N.J.: The Scarecrow Press, 1985), p. 45.

7. The Orpheus Club was a male choral society founded in 1872 by five members of the Abt Society. Originally they were under the direction of Michael Cross, giving concerts at the Musical Fund Hall. For more information on the Orpheus Club, see Gerson's Music in Philadelphia (Philadelphia, 1940), pp. 258-262.

8. Edward Bok was the successful Philadelphia publisher and editor of Ladies' Home Journal associated with the Curtis publishing empire through business and by marriage to Curtis' daughter Mary Louise.

9. Philadelphia Inquirer, October 20, 1958, obituary, page number deleted.

10. · See item 14 in bibliography: memorabilia of Frances McCollin.

11. The family was unclear as to what caused Frances' blindness. According to the record of

the Pennsylvania Institution for the Instruction of the Blind, the cause of blindness was ophthalmia neonatorum, a general heading used at the time for several eye problems, according to Dr. Michaile, Philadelphia ophthalmologist (interview, January 8, 1982). From the characteristics given in Frances McCollin's autobiography, Just Me, p. 11, it is his diagnosis that it was probably congenital glaucoma.

12. Frances McCollin, Just Me (unpublished autobiography, 1951, p. 18). See item 13 in bibliography: memorabilia of Frances McCollin.

13. See item 2 in bibliography: memorabilia of Frances McCollin.

14. "Frances McCollin Interview," The Diapason, August 1919, p. 12. Article found in Scrapbook I (see item 27A in bibliography: memorabilia of Frances McCollin).

15. Frances McCollin's home life at 927 Clinton Street included her mother, father, sister, as well as her two grandmothers McCollin and Lanigan, Uncle Ernest and Aunt Edith.

16. A bad experience with dogs during her early childhood discouraged Frances from ever wanting a seeing-eye dog. Instead, she was dependent upon others as guides when walking.

17. See bibliography, memorabilia of Frances McCollin. Housed by the Music Department of the Free Library of Philadelphia. The scores are catalogues in Chapter III of the dissertation.

18. The compositions done in Edward McCollin's hand include "Prelude and Variation on Chorale Fantasia in D minor," "Two Piano Duets after Diabelli," "June Song of Woodthrush," "Gypsy Dance," "Laus Deo," "Hymn Tunes of 1906-07."

19. Roma Angel, an organist and choirmaster at St. John's Lutheran Church, Elkins Park, was blind; Leslie Marles was crippled. The transcribers made no indication on the pieces they did and Leslie Marles could not identify his work in the interview claiming that his diabetic illness had caused him lapses of memory. He remembers transcribing during the period Stokowski was conducting the orchestra (1912-1938). As for Roma Angel's transcriptions, Frances McCollin says in an article referring to the "Adagio": "I dictate every note of all my compositions to my excellent writer Miss Roma Angel, FAGO." New Music Review, "Points and Counterpoints" (January 1934) found in Scrapbook 6 of Frances McCollin (see item 27F in bibliography: memorabilia of Frances McCollin).

20. Interview with Leslie Marles, Philadelphia, Pa., 10 June, 1981. By 1924, Frances and her mother had moved to 2128 Delancey Place.

21. Dr. William Timmings did copying for Frances between 1920 and 1922, Interview, September 4, 1981. Horatio Parker made suggestions on "Agnus Dei" in a letter to F. McCollin, 3 June 1908; "Into the Woods My Master Went" in a letter to F. McCollin, 5 June 1912, and "Berceuse," "The Lord Is King" in a letter to F. McCollin, 16 October, 1918. George Chadwick made corrections in the String Quartet in F in a letter to F. McCollin, 4 February 1925. Lucien Caillet made corrections on "Ring Out Wild Bells" in a letter to F. McCollin, 26 July, 1932 and 17 August 1938. Helen Leavitt made corrections on the "Doll's Lullaby" in a letter to F. McCollin, 2 January 1936. Gena Branscombe made suggestions on "Now is the Month of Maying," "Spring in Heaven," in a letter to F. McCollin, 1 May 1934. Gilchrist is mentioned as Frances' teacher in a newspaper article: Ledger, March 16, 1913, n.p., saved in Scrapbook I (see item 27A in bibliography: memorabilia of Frances McCollin).

22. Last Will and Testament, item 7 in bibliography: memorabilia of Frances McCollin.

23. "Notes made by Edward Garrett McCollin on musical interests and activities of his eldest daughter Frances McCollin born 927 Clinton Street, Philadelphia, October 24, 1892." See item 18 in bibliography: memorabilia of Frances McCollin.

24. Essay by Frances McCollin, p. 2. See item 3 in bibliography: memorabilia of Frances McCollin.

25. Notes made by Edward Garrett McCollin, p. 1. See item 18 in bibliography: memorabilia of Frances McCollin.

26. "Notes made by Edward Garrett McCollin," p. 6.

27. "Notes made by Edward Garrett McCollin," p. 7.

28. By 1897, since the McCollin family had moved to 2049 Upland Way, Overbrook, they travelled into the city by train. See Just Me, p. 12.

29. Interview with Dr. Arnett, Philadelphia, 17 November, 1979.

30. "Notes made by Edward Garrett McCollin," p. 4, p. 11.

31. "Notes made by Edward Garrett McCollin," p. 11.

32. Frances McCollin Essay, see item 2 in bibliography: memorabilia of Frances McCollin.

33. Helen Keller, The World I Live In (New York: Century Co., 1908), p. 109.

34. "Music Composer Since She Was Three," Philadelphia Inquirer, September 25, 1949, p. 14.

35. Just Me, p. 14. She slept in her crib even at three years of age.

36. Her imagination and love for fantasy gave direction to her musical ideas on these subjects. By her own admission she believed in fairies and Santa Claus.

37. Dorothy Mayer, "Frances McCollin, Pacifist Musician," Oct. 25, 1944 (English paper), p. 3. See item 2 in bibliography: memorabilia of Frances McCollin.

38. Guest Book, 2128 Delancey Place. See item 10 in bibliography: memorabilia of Frances McCollin.

39. Interview with Dr. Arnett, Philadelphia, 17 November, 1979.

40. Just Me, p. 37.

41. Interview with Dr. Arnett, Philadelphia, 17 November 1979.

42. Interview with Jeanne Behrend, Philadelphia, 9 April, 1980.

43. According to her autobiography, Just Me, she almost threw herself from a hotel bedroom window while in Maine.

44. Pennsylvania Institution for the Instruction of the Blind, Follow-Up Sheet. See item 2 in bibliography: memorabilia of Frances McCollin.

45. Just Me, p. 55.

46. Just Me, p. 21.

47. Just Me, p. 53.

48. W. Gilchrist to Edward McCollin, 14 March, 1913.

49. Just Me, p. 26.

50. ·Just Me, p. 52.

51. Just Me, p. 52.

52. Frances' father was born and raised a Baptist, but later joined the Episcopal Church.

53. Miss Maude Sproule also sang as a soloist at the Bethlehem Bach Festival, according to Frances' autobiography, Just Me, p. 53.

54. Just Me, p. 55.

55. Dorothy Mayer, "Frances McCollin, Pacifist Musician," October 25, 1944, English paper. p. 4. See item 2 in bibliography: memorabilia of Frances McCollin.

56. Interview with Jeanne Behrend, Philadelphia, 9 April, 1980. Perhaps she came by this propensity to pacifism naturally; one of her forebears had been a conscientious objector in the American Revolution and some descendants were Quaker according to genealogy charts prepared by George Scattergood in 1894. (See item 8 in bibliography: memorabilia of Frances McCollin.) Her mother was also active in anti-war organization.

57. On the sheet with "A Prayer to be used by those of the Draft Age," there is mention of peace committees Frances was associated with. See item 2 in bibliography: memorabilia of Frances McCollin.

58. John Tasker Howard, Our American Music (New York: T. Crowell Co., 1954), p. 495.

59. Manuscript Music Society, in 1916, "O Sing Unto the Lord"; Matinee Music Club, in 1918, The Singing Leaves; Society of Arts and Letters in 1918 for "Nights of Spring" and again in 1923 for "What Care I?"; National Federation of Music Clubs in 1919 for "The Midnight Sea" and honorable mention for the organ solo, "Caprice"; Mendelssohn Club, in 1921, for "Then Shall the Righteous Shine"; Strawbridge and Clothier Radio Competition, in 1925, for the radio peal, "Now the Day Is O'er"; Dayton Westminster Choir Award for the "Coming of June"; Sigma Alpha Iota in 1938 for "The Shepherds Had an Angel"; Eurydice Choral Award "Go Not Happy Day": Capital University in Columbus, Ohio in 1940, for "Peace I Leave with You"; Pennsylvania Federation of Music Clubs, in 1949, for "Christmas Bells"; Harvey Gaul Prize, in 1947, for "O Little Town of Bethlehem."

60. Public Ledger (March 30, 1918) n.p. (deleted). See item 27a in bibliography: memorabilia of Frances McCollin.

61. See item 25 in bibliography: memorabilia of Frances McCollin.

62. Entries of the catalogue include premier dates and performance locations of the compositions.

63. In the catalogue, mention is made of the pieces Frances dedicated to others. Works dedicated to Frances which are in the Music Library of the Free Library of Philadelphia include Johann Franco's "Elephants," "Intermezzo," and "First Born"; S. Marguerite Maitland's "Castles of Smiles--Suite for Piano"; Elisabeth Gest's "Dear Sirs Chorus," and Albert Dooner's "Short Prelude for Organ." See Item 3 in bibliography: memorabilia of Frances McCollin.

64. See item 4 in bibliography: memorabilia of Frances McCollin, for some of the correspondence of various people with F. McCollin which is in the music department of the Free Library of Philadelphia. Marian Anderson also gave Frances an autographed picture and wrote in her letter dated April 8, 1963, of the memorable walks she had with Frances in Rittenhouse Square. In her guest book of 2128 Delancey Place are autographs of people entertained in their home: singer Marian Anderson (December 13, 1938), Eugene Ormandy (October 11, 1938), and Eugene Zador (December 29, 1939).

65. That is why in the catalogue it is not uncommon to see repetitions of musical incipits for various pieces written for different instrumentation under various titles.

66. Evening Public Ledger, November 4, 1933, n.p. (deleted). See item 27F in bibliography.

67. See item 29 in bibliography: memorabilia of Frances McCollin.

68. Letter, Eugene Ormandy to Frances McCollin, 22 January 1940. See item 4D in bibliography: memorabilia of Frances McCollin.

69. Evening Bulletin, August 10, 1932, p. 11B.

70. Linton Martin, Philadelphia Inquirer, November 4, 1933, p. 13.

71. Linton Martin, Philadelphia Inquirer, January 10, 1929, n.p. (deleted). See item 27F in bibliography: memorabilia of Frances McCollin.

72. Used in pamphlet. See item 2 in bibliography: memorabilia of Frances McCollin.

73. Appendix C gives lists of talks.

74. No date or year can be found anywhere for this show. It only appears as an accomplishment in several résumés of Frances McCollin.

75. Teaching experience is listed in her résumé. See item 2 in bibliography: memorabilia of Frances McCollin.

76. See Appendix B for list of organizations.

77. Philadelphia Inquirer, September 25, 1949, p. 14.

78. Death Certificate of Frances McCollin. See item 7 in bibliography: memorabilia of Frances McCollin.

79. "Frances McCollin," obituary, New York Times, February 27, 1960, p. 19.

80. Public Ledger, March 30, 1918, p. 8.

Frances McCollin's creative output was not concentrated in one genre. In the vocal literature, she contributed 84 vocal pieces for children, 84 works for mixed chorus, 28 for women's chorus, 7 works for male chorus, and 20 works for vocal solo and duet. Instrumental works composed for individual instruments include 68 piano pieces (solo and duet), 12 organ pieces, one violin piece, one for violoncello, and one for organ and harp. Her works for larger groups include 18 orchestral selections, 2 for chorus and orchestra, and 8 chamber works. Whether the works were for large or small instrumental or vocal groups, Ms. McCollin seemed most comfortable composing works of small duration. The forms used for the vocal works, in particular those associated with the church service, were the chorale prelude, cantata, anthem, and carol from the German and English traditions of the Protestant Church. The orchestral literature includes many works in the nature of single movements, because of their brevity and titles such as "Adagio" and "Scherzo." Many times these orchestral works were also given titles that had programmatic significance. In fact, when they were performed, Frances McCollin usually wrote her own program notes telling the story behind the work. For example, the orchestral work, the "Scherzo" is subtitled "Heavenly Children at Play." According to the composer, it is the conception of the life hereafter of children, "continuing to play innocent games and pastimes of their earthly existence in greener playgrounds."[1]

Many of Frances McCollin's orchestral works are transcriptions of instrumental solo, vocal, and chamber repertoire, commissioned by people like Fabien Sevitzky. The "Adagio" for string orchestra was adapted from the String Quartette in F. The separate movements "Overture," "Chaconne," and "Sarabande" were originally written for string sextette under the title Suite in F, but then transcribed for string orchestra as separate pieces. The "Sarabande" movement of this suite was also transcribed as a solo piano piece. Other orchestral transcriptions were made from organ pieces, e.g., "All Glory, Laud and Honor," "Now All the Woods Are Sleeping," and "Cherubs at Play." The "Maypole Dance" was orchestrated from the original piano duet. Vocal works such as "A Prayer" originally for a cappella chorus were transcribed at the request of Fabien Sevitzky for string orchestra. Sometimes the composer made orchestrations of the accompaniments of songs for choral works like "Sleep Holy Babe" and "Ring Out Wild Bells." Many vocal works were first written for mixed chorus and then transcribed for women's voices, e.g., "Invitation," "The Shepherds Had an Angel," "Snowflakes," "Christmas Lullaby," "Come Hither Ye Faithful" and "It was a Lover and His Lass."

The literary texts of the vocal works were derived from various sources, including some of her own creations. The words of her songs "Ring Out Wild Bells," "Go Not, Happy Day," Sleeping Beauty cantata, and others are poems by Alfred Lord Tennyson. William Gilchrist, her teacher, had also used Tennyson as a source of text. Other literary texts selected were by Robert Louis Stevenson, Rudyard Kipling, Lewis Carroll, James Whitcomb Riley, all of whose works were read to Frances as a young girl. She also used the words of American authors with whom she was personally acquainted, such as Bertha Nutting and Bertha Ochsner, as well as nineteenth-century American poets like Mary Gardner Brainard (1837-1905) and William Walsham How (1823-1897). Many of her religious texts are taken directly from the Old and New Testaments. The words of the children's songs were written by the composer based on her life experiences, e.g., "A Bird Walk," "Going to the Zoo," "May Day," and family happenings, e.g., "Sister's Wedding," "Our Baby Sister." "Ahkoond of Swat" was her grandfather's poem, which she set to music.

It is important to understand that all the titles and texts of her secular and sacred works reflect the personality and life of Frances McCollin. Sound is used in association with visual ideas, such as The Singing Leaves, "The Shouting Sun," "Calm on the Listening Ear of Night," which may be an outcome of her blindness. Also the allusions to night in both titles and texts of the pieces "Nights O' Spring" and "At Eventide" may be associated with the fact that she lived in darkness all the time.

Her love of children is reflected in the numerous children's songs she chose to write, as well as the two cantatas, Pagliaccini and 'Twas the Night Before Christmas, her musical plays, Goldilocks and the Three Bears, Alice and the Calendar, and a children's opera, King Christmas. In fact, many of her songs were used in children's music books published by Ginn. Her own child-like loves for food, holidays, and games are obvious from her songs "Cream Puffs," "Chocolate Buds," "Ice Cream," "Christmas Shopping," "If I Were Toys" and "Games."

Her love of nature, in particular birds, is demonstrated by the numerous songs and instrumental pieces associated with birds by their title, such as "What Does Little Birdie Say," the vocal solo, "O Robin Little Robin," and "Bird Sings" for school orchestra (with no words), as well as many allusions made to birds in her songs about spring. Frances also enjoyed the changes of season, as reflected in the choral works, "Summer and Winter Days," "Spring," "Summer Showers," and "In the Bleak Midwinter."

Her involvement with pacifism was manifested not only in her joining peace organizations, but also in her choral works. "Today the Prince of Peace Is Born" and "Peace I Leave with You" were written and published during the time of World War II. These pieces communicated her pacifism to the world through her music.

Her discovery of religion at an early age spurred some of Frances' first compositions, such as the "Lamb of God." Many of the religious texts are associated with Christmas and Easter, two seasons of hope for Christians. It is interesting that she ends most of her sacred vocal works with the word "Amen" both in polyphonic ("Hail to the King of Glory") and homophonic ("Owe No Man Anything") styles even though the work is not always a hymn. Although the texts and titles are mostly of a rejoicing nature such as "He Is Risen," "The Lord Is King," there is also a sense of longing for the afterlife. Frances McCollin alludes to Christ's suffering for a better life through "The Way of the Cross" and "O Come and Mourn." These works convey the impression that she viewed this life as a passageway to the better world after death. In this life she felt she was only meant to serve and praise God through her music. Composers of the past often seemed to foresee their death by composing as their last work a requiem or a piece with the connotation of death. Frances McCollin's last composition, written in 1953, was titled "O Master Let Me Walk with Thee."

A general account of Frances McCollin's musical language follows, with specific musical examples from her works to illustrate various traits.

Frances McCollin's melodic gift is evident in all of her works, many of which are reminiscent of the sentimentality, characteristic of the lyrical melodies of Tschaikowsky. The composer borrowed many of her melodies from composers as divergent as Tschaikowsky and Bach. The opening melody of Tschaikowsky's song "Child Jesus Once a Garden Made" was used in her song "Into the Woods My Master Went."

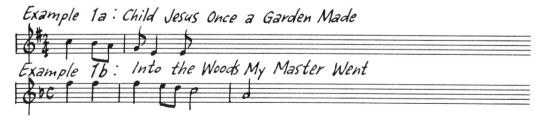

Example 1a: Child Jesus Once a Garden Made

Example 1b: Into the Woods My Master Went

Hymns and nursery rhyme tunes, important influences of her youth, are also evident in her works. Since she transcribed many of her own compositions, Frances McCollin borrowed the melodies from herself, developing them through various kinds of instrumentation and voicing.

The melodies are for the most part diatonic, and consist of small motifs, which like Ravel's, derive their identities from rhythm and pitch elements. The motives usually contain a jump of

a fourth or fifth.   One motif characterized by a jump of a fourth as well as its triplet figure
appears in several works:

Example: A: "Quintet" — B: "Sarabande"

This motif is repeated transformed and expanded to become the melodic line which is developed throughout a piece as in the "Sarabande."

Ms. McCollin uses another device for creating melodies, which was a favorite practice of
Robert Schumann.   In the "Prelude in A Minor," dedicated to Elisabeth Gittlen, the composer
uses the pitches corresponding to some of the letters in Miss Gittlen's name as her melody:
E-A-B-E-G-E- and elaborates on it.

Example : "Prelude in A minor"

Her melodies seem to move to the top of the range within the first eight measures.   They usually
follow a four measure pattern with sequential repetition or with a slight variation at the end.
In her vocal works the melodies follow the mood suggested by the words and are usually syllabic
in nature, with few melismas.   Word painting occurs on individual words such as "lengthen" in
"A Prayer," where the melody actually lengthens in duration.

Example : "A Prayer"

un —til the   sha-dows leng — then

In "Spring in Heaven," the entire melodic line is an example of word painting expressing
the ascent to heaven.

Example : "Spring in Heaven"

O when I get to   Heav'n I hope I'll find   Spring!

Sometimes a motif is connected with a set of words which occurs every time the words do. An example of this is in "O Come and Mourn" on the word "crucified":

Frances McCollin was well versed in nineteenth- and early twentieth century harmonic practices. Her "expressive" music tends to lean heavily on the French school, in particular Debussy and Ravel. In a newspaper article, Frances McCollin stated that Dr. Gilchrist made her appreciate the "moderns" by prescribing long practice hours of Debussy.[2] She uses the whole-tone scale in many of her pieces, as well as seventh and ninth chords, at times in succession. In the following example, "Hail to the King of Glory," the parallel blocks of sound gave an ethereal quality to the section and at the same time create tension through dissonance, which is also achieved by the presence of a double pedal point in the bass line. The use of the pedal point used by Debussy in "Fêtes," which elongates the supertonic harmony allowing several harmonies to pass above it, was an influence on Frances McCollin's works.

As for tonalities, her favorite was obviously F major, since most of her works are written in that key. The color she associated with F major was pink--a symbol of hope and happiness. It is therefore hardly surprising that it characterizes most of her works. But within that key, one finds Neapolitan relationships and other altered sixth chords which keep the interest and variety despite the overuse of the F tonality. Modulation is frequent in her works. At times, several key changes occur, to the point where she found it necessary in the "A Dream of the Christ Child" to change the key signature six times.

The American influence in her writing is evident in the ending to her pieces or important cadential points. She uses an altered V chord which can be labelled as a $V\sharp^7_5$ going to the tonic, a cadence used in much of the popular music or parlor music of the era:

In larger works of many movements, she employs the sonata-allegro form, as in the Quintette for piano and strings. Her sonata-allegro movements are somewhat similar to those of Beethoven and Brahms. The interplay between the highly formal structure and sentimental romantic lyricism suggests a Brahmsian quality. But her sonata-allegro movements, such as the opening one of the Quintette, do not show a real development of what has occurred thematically or harmonically. The recapitulation is a repetition verbatim of what was heard in the exposition. Miss McCollin makes use of cyclical treatment (like Beethoven) by reintroducing in the final movement of the Quintette the first theme of the opening movement.

In both the instrumental and vocal works McCollin combines homophony and polyphony, although the homophonic element seems more prominent. Her writings about the importance of hearing the text clearly, as well as her experiences with hymn writing, had a direct effect on her usage of many chord-like passages. The homophonic texture also gives the text a sense of declaration. Sometimes, in order to provide clarity to the literary text, she has only one voice part singing the words and the other parts humming.

Example : "Hail to the King of Glory"

Word painting is also "colored" by harmonic devices. In "Ring Out Wild Bells" the picture of bells is demonstrated at the beginning with an alternation of an F-minor chord and an E-flat minor chord.

Example : "Ring Out Wild Bells"

In Resurrection, the sustained chords for several bars go higher and higher symbolizing the rising of Christ.

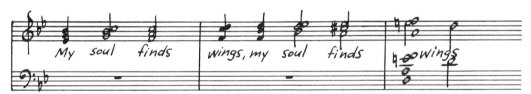

The tension of climactic points is heightened by dynamic markings of "FFF," at times, as in "Come Hither Ye Faithful" and pianissimo in the piece "A Prayer." But it is really the harmonic tension with use of dissonances, blocks of seventh chords, and modulations which add color to Miss McCollin's works and create drama in her composition. Even though the harmonies are progressive to an extent, she shows no traces of avant-garde characteristics such as atonality in her works.

Several of Frances McCollin's works are notated in the meters of 2/2 as in "Hail to the King of Glory" and Adagio; 5/4 as in the "A minor Prelude," and the Variations on an Original Theme for Piano and Orchestra; and 9/8 in "The Four Winds." Other works sometimes change in the course of the piece from 6/8 to 3/2 as in the trio of the "Scherzo." Syncopation is rarely to be found. An exception is in "Shouting Sun," where it is used to imitate Black music.

Certain rhythmic passages in the "Mother Goose Toccata" are programmatic. The rhythmic density suggests friends frolicking and scampering.

In her orchestral works, Frances McCollin does not deviate from standard instrumentation. Her full orchestra consists of piccolo, two flutes, two oboes, two bassoons, two horns, one trumpet, piano or percussion, and strings. She never stretches the ranges or fingerings of an instrument. She uses the woodwinds as melody instruments, especially in her Suburban Sketches and Bird Songs. She does not write for a heavy battery of percussion. At most, punctuation is provided by timpani, very much in the tradition of the Viennese classic orchestra. Her works for full orchestra notwithstanding, Miss McCollin seems to have had more facility writing for string orchestra, where she expertly handles divisi strings. In the "Adagio" for string orchestra, string sonorities, especially in the violoncellos and basses, are particularly effective. Pizzicati are also used skillfully.

In her vocal literature, Frances McCollin has written an approximately equal number of sacred and secular works for accompanied and unaccompanied voices. For her versatility in writing for different vocal ranges with expertise she was recognized during her lifetime. Many of her choral works for women's voices and mixed voices received awards.[3] Many of her mixed choral works are in eight parts and can be compared to her treatment of divisi strings in her orchestrations. In her vocal works, solo and choral often have an introduction two to four bars long, with a closing two to four bars after the vocal line is completed. The accompaniment supports the vocal lines, and often uses some of the sung motifs in an echo effect. The accompaniment of either piano or organ helps to enhance the dramatic possibilities of the song, whether it is a bell-like setting, as in "The Things of Everyday are all so Sweet" for solo voice and piano, or the fluttering air around "O Robin Little Robin." Many of her secular vocal works, both choral and solo, end with an ornamented tonic, as in "Grasshopper Green."

Frances McCollin was influenced by European musical ideas transmitted to her by her chief inspiration and example, her teacher, William Gilchrist. Many of the melodic, harmonic, rhythmic, and sound characteristics mentioned above are also prevalent in Gilchrist's works.[4] Even some of the titles of pieces are the same, such as "Ring out Wild Bells." It is said that imitation is the highest form of praise. But this uncritical and reverent imitation may have stifled the spark of imagination needed to individualize Frances McCollin's creation. Gilchrist died in 1916, the same year Frances started winning competitions for her musical compositions. Gilchrist left his student a legacy of education and Frances was to transmit the spirit of Gilchrist through her own compositions.

NOTES

1. See item 2 in bibliography: France McCollin program notes on Scherzo: "Heavenly Children at Play."

2. The Main Line (Ardmore, Pa.), September 18, 1931 p. 13 (in Scrapbook V).

3. See Appendix A for specific titles.

4. Martha Schleifer, "William Wallace Gilchrist: Life and Works," pp. 58-80.

There is a facet of Frances McCollin, not as yet discussed, which is an important link between her life and work.   Why were this woman's compositions well received during her lifetime?

In the study done by the Bureau of Musical Research in 1954 regarding musicians of Pennsylvania, New Jersey, and Delaware, Frances McCollin's biography was included among those of 12 women composers in the area.[1]   She was included in Who's Who in the East (1940-41) and her biography as a woman composer appeared in 13 printed sources.[2] Over 114 of her 333 compositions were shared with the public in 579 performances.   These compositions were part of liturgical services in churches, choral society concerts, symphony orchestra concerts, and organ, piano, and vocal recitals.   Ninety-three of her works were printed by 15 different publishing houses.   Her reputation extended to Warsaw (Poland), British Columbia, and Guatemala with the performances of her works by various orchestras there.   She also established a national distinction by winning 19 national competitions and having her works performed by the Philadelphia Orchestra and Indianapolis Symphony, among others.   She was not a stranger to the mass media with 17 performances of her works broadcast and used in films.[3] She had newspaper coverage from 1908 until her death in 1960, ranging from personal interviews to reviews of her works.   Recordings were made for both private and commercial use.

There were several fortunate circumstances that aided in the public reception of her music. Frances McCollin was living at a time when women composers were coming into their own.   She just missed being part of the mentality that "it was condescending to teach harmony and composition to women."[4]   One writer in 1902 observed that 50 years before, "the subject of harmony and counterpoint had been considered outside the province of women's education, and the acquisition of such knowledge, other than as a pastime, would have been regarded as a mental aberration."[5]   The change in attitude occurring at the turn of the twentieth century no longer regarded the woman composer as a cultural oddity.   As Fanny Morris Smith wrote in Etude magazine of September 1901:

> The first practical entrance of women into music as composers has been within the last twenty-five years....   Within this time women have been pressed into self support; colleges have been established; women have competed for and obtained university degrees; women dentists, lawyers, clergy, physicians, scientists, painters, architects, farmers, inventors and merchants, have all made their advent.   Side by side with them has arrived the woman composer.   She has come to stay.[6]

There was a need for choral music, in particular, due to the upsurge of musical societies and organizations that had developed from the beginning of the twentieth century.   According to the "Chamber of Commerce Report of 1917," there were over 250 permanent choral and operatic organizations in Philadelphia, not to mention the several orchestras like the Philadelphia Orchestra and the Philadelphia String Sinfonietta, which also had their origins in this century.[7] To encourage compositions to be written, many of the clubs sponsored competitions for original musical works, e.g., the Matinee Musical Club of Philadelphia, National Federation of Music Clubs, Eurydice Chorus of Philadelphia, and the Mendelssohn Club.   Clubs like the Philadelphia Music Club and the Manuscript Music Society set aside special days for performances of works written by club members.   These opportunities not only challenged Frances McCollin but directed the type of pieces that she wrote.

Ms. McCollin also took advantage of her family connection in Philadelphia musical circles. Since her father had helped found the Philadelphia Orchestra and her mother was active in the orchestra's women's committee, a close relationship with the orchestra's conductors and members was not surprising; it formed a positive force in getting Frances' music heard by the "right" people. In addition, her father's role as one of the founders of the Memorial Church of St. Paul, as well as his past experience as organist and choirmaster at the Central Presbyterian Church in Philadelphia, gave his daughter church connections for her sacred works to be performed. Many of the organists and choir directors of various churches, e.g., friends like Ralph Kinder, Roma Angel, and Rollo Maitland, had other connections with various societies, such as the American Guild of Organists, which gave them opportunities to perform solo recitals including Frances McCollin's works. Other loyal performers and composers, such as Elisabeth Gest and Vincent Persichetti, were associated with Etude magazine and the Theodore Presser Publishing Company, respectively; this gave Frances McCollin's works an outlet in print.

Frances' teachers not only opened the door to musical knowledge but also saw to it that her works were played by other students. Programs using her works were sponsored by organizations developed by her teachers. This is particularly true in the case of her teacher, William Gilchrist, whose influence and association with the Manuscript Music Society and the Philadelphia Music Club made it easier for Miss McCollin's work to be sponsored by them.[8]

Fabien Sevitzky, Frances McCollin's adopted Russian brother, was promoted by the McCollin family as a conductor. In turn, he chose to champion her music by performing her works with the various orchestras he conducted. He even commissioned her to transcribe some of her solo and chamber instrumental works for string and symphony orchestras. This, of course, increased her output.

Frances McCollin, on the other hand, being grateful to her friends, dedicated many of her works to individual performers such as Elisabeth Gest, Milton Kaye, Rollo Maitland, Fabien Sevitzky, as well as to societies like the Mendelssohn Club, and the National Federation of Music Clubs. Also, the McCollin family corresponded with publishing companies and sent résumés as well as music of Frances McCollin via Christmas cards and complimentary copies. Her involvement with various musical organizations, including those specifically for women, like the Matinee Musical Club, helped to promote her music, as well as that of other women composers.

Frances McCollin was at the right place at the right time and knew the right people. She was involved with many facets of music--composing, teaching, and performing--which opened many doors. These factors do not belittle her musical talent, since these "perfect" circumstances would have been meaningless if she had not written well-constructed and pleasing musical compositions. But it did give her an advantage over some of her contemporaries.

To call Frances McCollin a major figure in an epoch which boasted such a wealth of musical talent would be to claim too much. However, to have one's composed music in the repertoire of a major orchestra, along with works by Stravinsky, Tschaikowsky, Prokofieff, and Rachmaninoff is certainly no mean accomplishment. Critics of the era, certainly not noted for an excess of generosity, consistently praised the technical quality of her individual compositions and the totality of her contributions to the field of music. She was amply recognized by both the public and major musical personages of the time. Even in a period of tumultuous musical activity on the Philadelphia musical scene, Frances McCollin did not go unnoticed and can hardly be called a minor figure.

Technically, Frances McCollin's musical compositions are well above average. Her acceptance by distinguished composers, conductors, and critics of the time leaves little room to debate that point. In compositional technique, Frances McCollin followed a very conventional, traditional path and was of course influenced by her teachers and the popular musical currents of the time. However, Frances McCollin brought her own personal experiences and sensitivity to bear upon the themes of nature, religion, and childhood remembrances. She achieved in her works a higher aesthetic level of interpretation of these themes than did most composers of the period. Although Frances McCollin was not an innovator and did not introduce new thematic materials or techniques, she interpreted with extraordinary technical ability and aesthetic comprehension those elements that were in vogue in the music of the period.

NOTES

1. Spaeth, <u>Music and Dance in Pennsylvania, New Jersey, and Delaware</u>, p. 112.

2. Thirteen sources citing Frances McCollin are among the listed printed material in the bibliography.

3. See Appendix D: "Works of Frances McCollin Presented on Radio and Film."

4. Upton, <u>Woman in Music</u>, p. 12.

5. Adrienne Block, <u>Women in Music, Bibliography of Music and Literature</u>, p. xi.

6. Jeannie Pool, <u>Women in Music History, A Research Guide</u>, p. 4.

7. Gerson, <u>Music in Philadelphia</u>, p. 256.

8. Gerson, <u>Music in Philadelphia</u>, p. 250.

Lord support us all the day long of this troublous life
Until the shadows lengthen
And the evening comes, and the busy world is hushed
And the fever of life is over and our work is done
Then in Thy mercy, grant us a safe lodging
A holy holy rest, Thy holy rest and peace, at the last,
Through Jesus Christ our Lord, Amen.

"A Prayer"--Frances McCollin

Frances McCollin lived a life of faith and courage. Despite her handicap, she was willing to explore the full range of her potential in music by systematically pursuing a career as a composer and then promoting her works to share her creativity with the world. Frances became cognizant of her musical talent with the help of fine teachers such as her father, David Wood, H. Alexander Matthews, and William Gilchrist. Taking the responsibility of this God-given talent, she developed her skills through hard work, perseverance, and discipline, giving the world 333 creations of music. With the help of her family and friends, the world heard over 579 performances of those works.

Her exemplary life was an embodiment of music which gave her purpose to serve God and her fellow man. Through performances of her music, her expression of existence is perpetuated, and the spirit of Frances McCollin, Philadelphia heroine, survives.

This catalogue of Frances McCollin's works is an annotated compilation of all her printed and manuscript scores housed in the music department and the Fleisher Collection of the Free Library of Philadelphia. All her music has been donated to the Free Library by her family. The listing of her works is complete except for two manuscripts apparently mislaid by the family.

The catalogue consists of 333 works classified according to genre and listed in alphabetical order. The categories of works treated include chamber music, orchestral works, piano solos and duets, compositions for organ, organ and harp, violin, and violoncello; and vocal works ranging from solos and duets, unison children songs, cantatas, musical plays, children's opera, to choral works, both secular and sacred, for male voices, female voices, and full chorus.

This catalogue follows the format and methodology of the Edwin A. Fleisher Music Collection Catalogue, in the application of which I have been immeasurably assisted by Sam Dennison, then curator of the Fleisher Collection and compiler of its latest catalogue volume.

In those instances where it was necessary to deviate somewhat from the Fleisher model, because of certain peculiarities or circumstances of an individual work, these deviations from the norm are noted in the entry.

ABBREVIATIONS

Cataloguing Information

†	Prize-winning composition
*	Works to be noted by listeners and performers
ADM	Folder identification: Annette DiMedio, catalogue of Frances McCollin's works
CM	classification: chamber music
ChO	orchestral-choral
SchO	school orchestra
StrO	string orchestra
Sym	symphony orchestra
PS	solo piano
PD	piano-four hands
O	solo organ
OH	organ and harp
VI	solo violin, piano accompaniment
VC	solo violoncello, piano accompaniment
U	children's voices--unison, piano accompaniment
UD	children's voices--unison, piano-four hands
D	children's voices--duet
F	children's voices--four-part
UC	children's voices--cantata
MP	children's voices--musical play
AW	children's voices--song cycle "Alice in Wonderland"
KC	children's voices--opera
V	solo vocal
H	sacred choral, a cappella

HA	sacred choral, accompanied
FIN	sacred choral, cantata, accompanied
SUM	secular choral, a cappella
SAC	secular choral, accompanied
WS	sacred choral: women's voices a cappella
WW	sacred choral: women's voices accompanied
LUS	secular choral: women's voices, a cappella
LASS	secular choral: women's voices, accompanied
LAS	secular choral-cantata: women's voices, accompanied
MC	secular choral: male voices, a cappella
MA	secular choral: male voices, accompanied

Instruments

Picc	piccolo
Fl	flute
Ob	oboe
E.H.	English horn
Cl	clarinet
Bn	bassoon
Sax	saxophone
Hn	horn
Tpt	trumpet
Tbn	trombone
Tuba	tuba
B.Dr.	bass drum
S.Dr.	snare drum
T.Dr.	tenor drum
Timp	timpani
Cast	castanets
Cym	cymbals
Tamb	tambourine
Xyl	xylophone
Gong	gong
Trgl	triangle
Pno	piano
Cemb	cembalo
Hpsch	harpsichord
Org	organ
Cel	celesta
Hp	harp
S	soprano
A	alto
T	tenor
Bar	baritone
B	bass
Str	strings
Vn	violin
Va	viola
Vc	violoncello
Cb	contrabass

Abbreviations

General

acc	accompaniment
c	copyright
Ms	manuscript
no	number
orch	orchestra
op	opus
p	page
Tr	translation

INSTRUMENTAL: CHAMBER MUSIC

ADM 1 CM-1. Chorale Prelude and Chaconne for Society of Ancient Instruments: Ye Watchers
and Ye Holy Ones (10')

Vn. I, Vn. II, Va., Vc., Pno./Ms./Score 20p./Composed: March 20, 1938, to July 9, 1938/
Arrangement for chorus: see ADM 66 HA-25.

ADM 1 CM-2. Diversion. Wind quintette (5')

Fl., Ob., Cl., Hn., Bn./Ms./Score 12p./Composed January 3, 1943, to February 2, 1943./First
perf.: Philadelphia Woodwind Quintet, Bryn Mawr, Pa., October 30, 1963.

ADM 2 CM-3. Fantasia. String quartette (17')

Vn. I, Vn. II, Va., Vc./Ms./Score 52p. [parts available]./Possible composition dates: September 9, 1935-July 26, 1936./Sent to Pheta A. Sooland Award Competition on March 28, 1962 under pen name "Karlton."

*ADM 4 CM-4. Quintette in F Major. Piano, two violins, viola, and violoncello. 1. Allegro moderato. 2. Lento. 3. Allegretto scherzando. 4. Presto (27')

Vn. I, Vn. II., Va., Vc., Pno./Ms./Score 132p. [parts available]./Composed for and submitted to the Competition of the Musical Fund Society, 1927./Pen name "Atticus" used by Frances McCollin./First perf.: Jordan Conservatory Quintette, Phila., Pa., May 8, 1942.

ADM 9 CM-6. String Quartette in F Major. 1. Allegro Moderato. 2. Andante. 3. Scherzo. 4. Finale (20')

Vn. I, Vn. II, Va., Vc./Ms./Score 160p. [parts available]./Date beginning composition: June 7, 1920.

ADM 8 CM-5. Suite in F. String sextette. 1. Overture. 2. Pavane. 3. Minuet. 4. Sarabande.
  5. Gigue (24')

Vn. I, Vn. II, Va. I, Va. II, Vc. I, Vc. II./Ms./Score 82p. [parts available]./Dates of composition: 1. Overture: July 11, 1931–June 7, 1932. 2. Pavane: June 23, 1932–July 11, 1932.
3. Minuet: July 4, 1932–July 11, 1932. 4. Sarabande: June 16, 1932./Arrangement for symphony:
see ADM30 Sym-8; string orchestra: see ADM 22 Str O-6.

ADM 10 CM-7. Theme and Variations. Woodwind quintette

Fl., Ob., Cl., Hn., Bn./Ms./Score 44p. [parts available]./Composed: December 11, 1953, to
March 11, 1954.

ADM 1 CM-1. Ye Watchers and Ye Holy Ones. See: Chorale Prelude [and Chaconne] for Society
  of Ancient Instruments

INSTRUMENTAL: ORCHESTRAL-CHORAL

ADM 13 ChO-2. August. See: Suburban Sketches

ADM 13 ChO-2. June. See: Suburban Sketches

ADM 12 ChO-1. "Ring Out Wild Bells." Words by Alfred Tennyson (10')

Picc., 2 Fl., 2 Ob., E.H., 2 Cl., B.Cl., 2 Bn., Cb. Cl., Sax-2 Hn., 2 Tpt., 2 Tbn., 1 Tuba-
Timp., Perc.-Pno., Org., Cel., Hp.-SATB [Chorus]-Str./Ms./Score 64 p. [parts available]./
Arrangement for chorus: See ADM 65 HA 19 and HA 20.

ADM 13 ChO-2. Suburban Sketches for Orchestra. Pt. 1. June. I. Morning. II. Mid Day.
   III. Evening. Pt. 2. August. I. Morning. II. Mid Day. III. Evening (30')

Picc., 4 Fl., 2 Ob., E.H., 4 Cl., 4 Bn.-4 Hn., 4 Tpt., 2 Tbn.-Timp., Perc.-Pno./cel.-3 children
choruses-Str./Ms./Score 168p./Composed: April 25, 1936-June 17, 1936./Arrangement of "June"
for women's chorus; see ADM 75 LAS-2; of "August" for piano-four hands. With words: see
ADM 37 PD2, ADM 98 UD-1.

INSTRUMENTAL: SCHOOL ORCHESTRA

ADM 15 SchO-1. Bird Songs. Three easy pieces for elementary-school orchestra (6')

   1. The Robin's Evening Song

2. Meadow Larks.

3. Two Wood Thrushes.

Picc., 2 Fl., 2 Ob., 2 Bn.-2 Hn., 1 Tpt., 2 Tbn.-Pno. (or Cel.)-Str./Ms./Score 28p./Completion of "The Robin's Evening Song"--March 2, 1941./Completion of "Meadow Larks"--March 2, 1941./Arrangement of "Bird Songs" for Piano duet: See: ADM 37 PD-7, ADM 38 PD-10, ADM 38p. 2-14.

ADM 16 SchO-2.   "Grandma Grunts."   Children's song arranged for string orchestra

Vn. I, Vn. II, Va., Vc., Cb.-Str. Orch./Ms./Score 12p. [parts available]./Arrangement for children's voices: see ADM 49 U-60.

ADM 17 SchO-3. Maypole Dance. Intermediate-school orchestra (5')

Picc., 2 Fl., 2 Ob., 2 Cl., 2 Bn.-4 Hn. 2 Tpt., 2 Tbn.-Timp., Perc.-Pno. or Cel.-Str./Ms./
Score 32p./Date of completion: April 17, 1941./Arrangement for piano duet: see ADM 37 PD-6.

ADM SchO-1. Meadow Larks. See: Bird Songs

ADM SchO-1. Robin's Evening Song. See: Bird Songs

ADM SchO-1. Two Wood Thrushes. See: Bird Songs

INSTRUMENTAL: STRING ORCHESTRA

*ADM 18 Str O-1. Adagio. Arranged for string orchestra from String Quartette in F Major

Vn. I, Vn. II, Va., Vc., Cb.-Str. Orch./Carl Fischer, © 1933./Score 24p. [parts available,
piano reduction]./Arrangement for the Sinfonietta, Fabien Sevitzky, conductor, 1927./Dedicated
to the memory of McCollin's father./First perf.: Philadelphia Chamber Sinfonietta, Haddonfield,
N.J., Oct. 18, 1927.

ADM 19 Str O-2. All Glory, Laud, and Honor. See: Chorale Prelude. All Glory, Laud, and
Honor

*ADM 19 Str O-2. Chorale Prelude, All Glory, Laud and Honor

Vn. I, Vn. II, Va., Vc., Cb.-Str. Orch./G. Riccordi and Co., © 1941./Score 10p. [parts avail-
able.]/Arrangement for organ: see ADM 39 O-1./Transcription commissioned by the Philadelphia
Chamber String Sinfonietta, 1936, transcription, 1937./First perf.: Philadelphia Chamber String
Sinfonietta, Philadelphia, Pa., April 20, 1938.

*ADM 19 Str O-3. Chorale Prelude. Now All the Woods Are Sleeping (3')

Vn. I, Vn. II, Va., Vc., Cb.-Str. Orch./G. Riccordi and Co., © 1941./Score 7p. [parts avail-
able]./In Fleisher Collection 1741S./Arrangement for organ, 1935: see ADM 40 O-9./Transcribed
1936./Intended as part of a larger work, Suburban Sketches./First perf.: Philadelphia Chamber
String Sinfonietta, Philadelphia, Pa., April 20, 1938.

*ADM 21 Str O-4. Heavenly Children at Play. Scherzo for string orchestra (8')

Vn. I, Vn. II, Va., Vc., Cb.-Str. Orch./Ms./Score 36p. [parts available]./Also in Fleisher
Collection 2308S./Written for and dedicated to Philadelphia Chamber Sinfonietta, Fabien Sevitzky./
First perf.: Philadelphia Chamber String Sinfonietta, Philadelphia, Pa., Jan. 9, 1929.

ADM 19 Str O-3. Now All the Woods Are Sleeping. See: Chorale Prelude. Now All the Woods
    Are Sleeping

ADM 22 Str O-5. A Prayer

Vn. I, Vn. II, Va., Vc., Cb.-Str. Orch./Ms./Score 4p. [parts available]./Also in Fleisher
Collection 1734S./Transcription commissioned by the Philadelphia Chamber String Sinfonietta,
1930./Dedicated to Fabien Sevitzky./Arranged for chorus, 1930. See ADM 61H-21./First perf.:
Philadelphia String Sinfonietta, Philadelphia, Pa., March 13, 1933.

ADM 21 Str O-4. Scherzo. Heavenly Children at Play. See: Heavenly Children at Play

ADM 22 Str O-6. Suite for Strings (15')

    1. Overture

    2. Sarabande

3. Chaconne in F minor

Vn. I, Vn. II, Va., Vc., Cb.-Str. Orch./Ms./Score 45p. [parts available]./Also in Fleisher Collection 2076S./Composed: May 26, 1940-June 12, 1940./First two movements transcribed from Suite in F, 1940./Pen name "Dionne" used.

INSTRUMENTAL: SYMPHONY ORCHESTRA

ADM 23 Sym-1.   Chorale Prelude on "I Wonder as I Wander"

2 Fl., 2 Ob., 1 E.H., 2 Cl., 2 Bn.-4 Hn., 2 Tpt., 2 tbn.-Timp.-Cel., Hp.-Str./Ms./Score 24p. [parts available]./Date of completion: August 17, 1945./Pen name "Selin" used./First perf.: Indianapolis Symphony, Indianapolis, Indiana, Nov. 27, 1948.

ADM 24 Sym-3.   Christmas Poem

Picc., 2 Fl., 2 Ob., 1 E.H., 2 Cl., 2 Bn. C. Bn.-4 Hn., 2 Tpt., 2 Tbn.-Timp.-Cel., Hp.-Str./ Ms./Score 59p./Composed: March 2, 1940, to Nov. 10, 1940./Dedicated to Fabien Sevitzky./First perf.: Dec. 13, 1940.

ADM 25 Sym-4.   Madrigal for Flute and Orchestra   (10')

Picc., 2 Fl., 2 Ob., E.H., 2 Cl., 2 Bn.-4 Hn., 2 Tpt., 2 Tbn.-Timp.-Cel., Hp.-Solo Fl. Solo
Vn.-Str./Ms./Score 60p./Composed: Aug. 23, 1941, to Oct. 26, 1941.

ADM 26 Sym-5.   Nocturne   (12')

2 Fl., 2 Ob., 2 Cl., 2 Bn.-4 Hn., 2 Tpt., 2 Tbn.-Timp., Perc.-Cel., Hp.-Solo Vn.-Str./Ms./
Score 44p./Composed: June 13, 1934, to Aug. 10, 1940./First perf.: Town Hall Club, New York,
May 6, 1951.

ADM 27 Sym-6.   Nursery Rhyme Suite.   1. Playing Games.   2. Nap Time.   3. The Two Pies.
   4. Mother Goose Animal   (10')

2 Fl., 2 Ob., 2 Cl., 2 Bn.-4 Hn., 2 Tpt., 2 Tbn.-Timp., Perc.-Hp. Cel.,-Str./Ms./Score 118p.
[parts available]./Dates of composition: First movement: July '39 to Feb. 10, 1940./Second movement: Dec. 15, 1939 to Mar. 23, 1940./Third movement: Mar. 10, 1940./Fourth movement:
Jan. 7, 1940, to Feb. 10, 1940./Arrangement of "Toccata" for piano: see ADM 34 PS-28./First
perf.: Philadelphia Orchestra. Philadelphia, Pa., Mar. 31, 1951.

ADM 29 Sym-7. Scherzo and Fugue in C Minor (13')

Picc., 2 Fl., 2 Ob., 2 Cl., 2 Bn.-4 Hn., 2 Tpt., 2 Tbn.-Timp., Perc., Hp.-Str./Ms./Score 70p. [parts available]./Scherzo composed: Nov. 7, 1944, to Mar. 24, 1945./Fugue composed: Mar. 27, 1945, to Jan. 3, 1946./Leslie Marles copyist; Fabien Sevitzky did corrections.

ADM 30 Sym-8. Suite in F. Full orchestra (25')

   1. Overture

   2. Pavane

   3. Minuet

   4. Sarabande

5. Fugue

2 Fl., 2 Ob., 2 Cl., 2 Bn.-2 Hn., 2 Tpt.,-Timp., Perc.-Hp. Cel.-Str./Ms./Score 198p. [piano reduction]./Also in Fleisher Collection 3104, 3105, 3106, 3107, 3108./First perf.: Orchestra Society, Philadelphia, Pa., April 1, 1934.

ADM 31 Sym-9.   Variations on an Original Theme for Piano and Orchestra

2 Fl., 2 Ob., 2 Cl., 2 Bn.-2 Hn., 3 Tpt., 2 Tbn.-Timp.-Pno. [solo instrument]-Str./Ms./ Score 74p./Composed: Nov. 28, 1941, to May 17, 1942./Dedicated to Milton Kaye./First perf.: Wallenstein Sinfonietta, Philadelphia, Pa., Apr. 13, 1943.

INSTRUMENTAL: SOLO PIANO

ADM 33 PS-14.   At the Court Ball.   See: Gavotte

ADM 32 PS-1.   Bedtime Story

Solo pno./Ms./Score 2p./Date of completion: June 4, 1938.

ADM 32 PS-2.   Berceuse for Barbara

Solo pno./Ms./Score 8p./Dedicated to Barbara Stonorov.

ADM 32 PS-3.   The Big Fly

Solo pno./Ms./Score 2p./Composed Sept. 13, 1940, to Sept. 19, 1940.

ADM 32 PS-5.   Can't Catch Me

Solo pno./Ms./Score 4p.

ADM 32 PS-6.   Chorale Prelude on "Hatikvah"

Solo pno./Ms./Score 8p./Date of completion: Aug. 26, 1952.

ADM 32 PS-7.   Dance for Derek

Solo pno./Ms./Score 8p./Date of completion: Mar. 16, 1946.

ADM 32 PS-8.   Daydreaming

Solo pno./Ms./Score 2p./Begun Mar. 18, 1946, but incomplete.

ADM 32 PS-9.   The Dolls' Ball

Solo pno./Ms./Score 2p./Completed Dec. 20, 1939.

ADM 33 PS-10.   The Dripping Faucet

Solo pno./Galaxy Music Corp., © 1948./Score 4p./Dedicated to Carolyn Foster.

ADM 33 PS-11.   Duettino or Little Duet (Canon on the Fourth).   Easy piano solo

Solo Pno./Ms./Score 4p./Date of completion: May 29, 1935./Dedicated to Alice Luba Monasevitch./
One of pieces chosen for "Style of Bach Series."

ADM 33 PS-12.   Follow the Leader.   Easy piano piece

Solo pno./Ms./Score 4p./Pen name "Garrett" used.

ADM 33 PS-13.   Funny Fantasia on "Baa Baa Black Sheep" and "The Merry Farmer"

Solo pno./Ms./Score 10p./Composed Aug. 3, 1943, to Aug. 31, 1943./Dedicated to Richard Foster.

ADM 33 PS-14.   Gavotte.   Piano solo [At the Court Ball]

Solo pno./Ms./Score 4p./Completion date: Sept., 1934./Dedicated to Gregory Barish Votaw./
One of pieces chosen for "Style of Bach Series."

ADM 33 PS-15.   Gigue.   Piano solo

Solo pno./Ms./Score 4p./Pen name "Garrett" is used.

ADM 33 PS-17.   Gypsy Dance

Solo pno./G. Schirmer Inc., © 1925./Score 2p./Date of completion: Aug., 1904./First perf.:
Pupils of Mary E. Anderson, Philadelphia, Pa., May 11, 1940.

ADM 33 PS-18.   Hoop-Rolling

Solo pno./Ms./Score 4p.

ADM 33 PS-19.   Hopping

Solo pno./Ms./Score 20p.

ADM 33 PS-20. Hop, Skip, and Jump. Piano solo

Solo pno./Ms./Score 2p./Completed Dec. 20, 1937.

ADM 33 PS-21. In the Clock Shop at Three. Piano

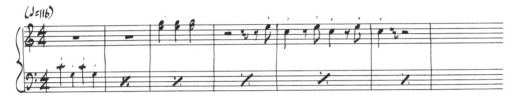

Solo pno./Harold Flammer Inc., © 1940./Score 4p./Dedicated to Alice Frances Arnett.

ADM 33 PS-11. Little Duet. See: Duettino

ADM 34 PS-22. March of the Toys

Solo pno./Ms./Score 4p./Composed Oct. 1, 1939, to Nov. 25, 1939.

ADM 33 PS-23. Merry Marita

Solo pno./Harold Flammer Inc., © 1940./Score 2p./Date of completion: May 11, 1940./Dedicated to Marita Mullan.

ADM 34 PS-24.   Mine Own Minuet

Solo pno./Ms./Score 2p./Incomplete.

ADM 34 PS-25.   Minuet

Solo pno./Harold Flammer Inc., © 1940./Score 12p.

ADM 34 PS-26.   Minuet [Petit]

Solo pno./Ms./Score 4p./Dedicated "To John Hancock Arnett, Jr."/Same as piece titled "Minuet."/
Part 2 of "Styles of Bach Series."

ADM 34 PS-27.   Molly's Minuet

Solo pno./Ms./Score 4p./Completed Sept. 13, 1940.

ADM 33 PS-16. Mother and Daddy. Easy piano piece

Solo pno./Ms./Score 4p.

ADM 34 PS-28. Mother Goose Toccata

Solo pno./Ms./Score 8p./Composed Oct. 1, 1939-Oct. 15, 1939./First perf.: Elisabeth Gittlen, Philadelphia, Pa., Mar. 20, 1944.

ADM 34 PS-26. Petit Minuet. See: Minuet [Petit]

ADM 34 PS-30. Playtime

Solo pno./Ms./Score 4p./Date of completion: Aug. 15, 1941.

ADM 35 PS-31. Prelude in A minor

Solo pno./Ms./Score 4p./First perf: Elisabeth Gittlen, Philadelphia, Pa., Mar. 20, 1944.

ADM 35 PS-32.   Piano Prelude in A-Flat Major

Solo pno./Ms./Score 4p./First perf.:   Elisabeth Gittlen, Philadelphia, Pa., May 4, 1944.

ADM 35 PS-33.   Prelude in C Minor

Solo pno./Ms./Score 4p.

ADM 35 PS-35.   Prelude in D for Piano

Solo pno./Xerox/Score 8p.

ADM 35 PS-35.   Prelude in D-Flat

Solo pno./Score 4p./In ink./First perf.:   Anya Lawrence, Philadelphia, Pa., Oct. 14, 1979.

ADM 35 PS-36.   Prelude in E Minor

Solo pno./Ms./Score 6p./Begun Feb. 11, 1946; incomplete.

ADM 35 PS-37. Promenade

Solo pno./Ms./Score 4p.

ADM 35 PS-38. Rain on the Leaves

Solo pno./Ms./Score 2p./Date of completion: Jan. 30, 1938.

ADM 79 PS-39. Rondo for Piano

Solo pno./Ms./Score 3p./Arrangement for organ: See ADM 40 D-12.

*ADM 35 PS-40. Sarabande. Piano solo (3")

Solo pno./Ms./Score 8p./Sarabande transcription from "Suite in F" (fourth movement)/First perf.: Jeanne Behrend, Philadelphia, Pa., Mar. 12, 1939.

ADM 32 PS-4.   Sicilienne

Solo pno./Ms./Score 2p./Date of completion: Dec. 20, 1937.

ADM 36 PS-41.   Sonatina

Solo pno./Ms./Score 4p./Begun Aug. 5, 1951; incomplete.

ADM 36 PS-42.   Springboard

Solo pno./Ms./Score 2p./Completed June 4, 1938.

ADM 36 PS-43.   Tom, Tom the Piper's Son.   Piano solo

Solo pno./Ms./Score 4p.

ADM 36 PS-44. Tune for Tina

Solo pno./Ms./Score 6p./Composed: Feb. 23, 1946.

ADM 36 PS-45.   "Upside Down" Overture.   Piano solo

Solo pno./Ms./Score 4p./Dedicated to Albert Nicholson./Also listed on title page as "No. 1 Style of Bach Series."

ADM 36 PS-46.   Water Wheel

Solo pno./Ms./Score 4p./Date of completion: Nov. 25, 1939./Pen name "Wheelright" used.

ADM 36 PS-47.   What Time Is It? A Musical Puzzle

Solo pno./Ms./Score 4p.

INSTRUMENTAL: PIANO-FOUR HANDS

ADM 37 PS-1.   Around the Block and Home Again

Pno.-four hands./Ms./Score 2p./Date of completion: Nov. 29, 1948.

ADM 37 PS-2.   August

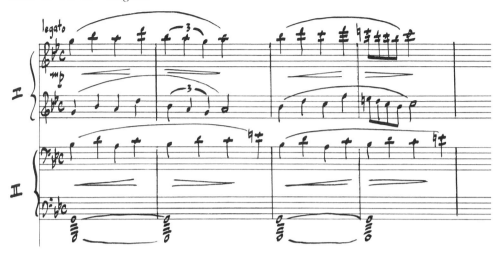

Pno.-four hands./Ms./Score 8p./Date of completion: Apr. 29, 1937.

ADM 37 PD-3.   Canoeing

Pno.-four hands./Ms./Score 6p./Arrangement for children's voices: see ADM 50 D-1.

ADM 37 PD-4.   The Cuckoo Clock

Pno.-four hands./Ms./Score 4p.

ADM 37 PD-5.   Letting the Old Cat Die

Pno.-four hands./Ms./Score 4p./Date of completion: May 12, 1937./Arrangement for children's voices: See ADM 78 UD-2.

ADM 37 PD-6.   Maypole Dance

Pno.-four hands./Ms./Score 12p./Date of completion: Sept. 19, 1940./First perf.:   Annette and Regina DiMedio, Philadelphia, Pa., May 17, 1981.

ADM 37 PD-7.   Meadow Larks

Pno.-four hands./Ms./Score 2p.

ADM 37 PD-8.   Off to the Woods

Pno.-four hands./Ms./Score 4p./Arrangement for children's voices: see ADM 46 U-32,
ADM 78 UD-4.

ADM 37 PD-9.   The Phoebe Bird

Pno.-four hands./Ms./Score 4p./Date of completion: Oct. 5, 1948.

ADM 38 PD-10.   The Robin's Evening Song.   Piano duet at one piano

Pno.-four hands./Ms./Score 8p./Composed: Aug. 13, 1939, to Nov. 13, 1938.

ADM 38 PD-11.   Shower

Pno.-four hands./Ms./Score 8p./Composed: Jan. 4, 1941, to Apr. 6, 1941./First perf.:
Annette and Regina DiMedio, Philadelphia, Pa., May 17, 1981.

ADM 38 PD-12.   A Summer Afternoon

Pno.-four hands./Ms./Score 12p./Date composition begun: Oct. 3, 1942 (incomplete).

ADM 38 PD-13.   Two Piano Duets After the Style of Studies by Diabelli

Pno.-four hands./Ms./Score 4p./Date of completion: Apr., 1900./Transcribed by Edward
Garrett McCollin.

ADM 38 PD-14.   Two Wood Thrushes.   Easy duet for piano

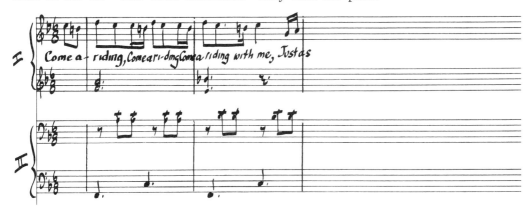

Pno.-four hands./Ms./Score 4p./Date of completion: June 20, 1937.

INSTRUMENTAL: SOLO ORGAN

*ADM 39 O-1.   All Glory, Laud, and Honor.   Chorale prelude for organ   (5')

Org. solo./G. Riccordi and Co., © 1941./Score 7p./First perf.:   Richard Purvis, Pottsville, Pa.,
Apr. 17, 1941.

*ADM 79 O-2.   Berceuse.   Organ

Org. solo./Oliver Ditson Co., © 1918./Score 6p./Completion: Nov. 1916./First perf.:   Frances
McCollin, Philadelphia, Pa., Apr. 1917.

*ADM 39 O-3. Canzonetta. Organ (8'30")

Org. solo./The Boston Music Co., © 1921./Score 5p./Dedicated to Mrs. George C. Thomas./
First perf.: Ralph Kinder, Philadelphia, Pa., Jan. 15, 1925.

*ADM 39 O-4. Cherubs at Play. Organ

Org. solo./H. W. Gray Co., © 1926./Score 7p./Dedicated to and played by Rollo F. Maitland./
First perf.: Frances McCollin, Philadelphia, Pa., Feb. 12, 1922.

ADM 40 O-13. Cherubs at Play or Allegretto Scherzando. Organ, flute, harp, violin, and
    violoncello

Org. (Hp., Fl., Vn., Vc.-obbligato)./Ms./Score 14p.

ADM 39 O-1. Chorale Prelude, All Glory, Laud, and Honor. See: All Glory, Laud, and Honor.

ADM 40 O-8. Chorale Prelude for Organ on "I Wonder as I Wander"

Org. solo./Ms./Score 6p./Date of completion: Dec. 8, 1945./The pen name Jacobson is used.

ADM 40 O-9.   Chorale Prelude for Organ.   Now All the Woods Are Sleeping

Org. solo./G. Riccordi & Co., © 1941, © 1950./Score 5p./First perf.:   Roma Angel, Valley Forge, Pa., Nov. 25, 1950.

ADM 39 O-5.   Christmas Fantasia.   Organ   (10')

Org. solo./Ms./Score 28p./First perf.:   Clarabel G. Thomson, Philadelphia, Pa., Apr. 22, 1941.

ADM 39 O-6.   Duetto for Organ

Org. solo./Ms./Score 8p./Pen names "William" and "Canonicus" are used./First perf.:   St. Michael's Evangelical Lutheran Church, Philadelphia, Pa., Oct. 11, 1925.

ADM 40 O-7. Fantasia in D Minor. Organ

Org. solo./Ms./Score 20p.

ADM 40 O-8. I Wonder as I Wander. See: Chorale Prelude on "I Wonder as I Wander."

ADM 40 O-9. Now All the Woods Are Sleeping. See: Chorale Prelude for Organ. Now All the Woods Are Sleeping.

ADM 40 O-10. Pastorale. Organ

Org. solo./Ms./Score 8p.

ADM 40 O-11. Prelude and Variations on a Chorale. Organ

Org. solo./Ms./Score 12p./Piece based on "Ach Gott und Herr, wie gross und schwer sind mein begange Sunden."

*ADM 40 O-12. Rondo. Organ

Org. solo./Oliver Ditson Co., © 1920./Score 5p./First perf.: Harry Banks, Philadelphia, Pa.,
Mar. 3, 1918.

INSTRUMENTAL: ORGAN AND HARP

ADM 41 OH-1. Pavane. Organ and harp

Org., Hp./Ms./Score 4p./First perf.: Unitarian Church, Germantown, Pa., Aug. 24, 1951.

INSTRUMENTAL: SOLO VIOLIN, PIANO ACCOMPANIMENT

ADM 79 VI-1. In Fairyland. Dance of the Midgets. Violin and piano

Vn., Pno. acc./Theodore Presser Co., © 1928./Score 4p./Edited by Lucius Cole./First perf.:
Philadelphia Musical Club, Composer's Day, Philadelphia, Pa., Jan. 27, 1920.

ADM 79 VI-2.   In Fairyland.   The Fairies' Dream.   Reverie for violin and piano

Vn., Pno. acc./Theodore Presser Co., © 1929./Score 3p./Edited by Lucius Cole./First perf.: Philadelphia Musical Club, Composer's Day, Philadelphia, Pa., Jan. 27, 1920.

ADM 42 VI-3.   In Fairyland.   Minuet.   Violin and piano

Vn., Pno. acc./Theodore Presser Co., © 1929./Score 5p./First perf.: Philadelphia Musical Club, Composer's Day, Philadelphia, Pa., Jan. 27, 1920.

ADM 79 VI-4.   In Fairyland.   A Game of Tag--Perpetual Motion.   Violin and piano

Vn., Pno. acc./Theodore Presser Co., © 1929./Score 6p./First perf.: Philadelphia Musical Club, Composer's Day, Philadelphia, Pa., Jan. 27, 1920.

INSTRUMENTAL: SOLO VIOLONCELLO, PIANO ACCOMPANIMENT

ADM 43 VC-1.   Spanish Dance.   Violoncello and piano

Vn., Pno. acc./Ms./Score 12p./Completion: July 22, 1942./Dedicated to Delphine Desip.

VOCAL: CHILDREN'S VOICES--UNISON, PIANO ACCOMPANIMENT

ADM 44 U-1.   Airplane.   Words by Frances McCollin

Children's Voices--unison, Pno. acc./Ms./Score 6p./Completion date: July 26, 1943.

ADM 44 U-2.   All About Andrea.   Words by Frances McCollin

Children's Voices--unison, Pno. acc./Ms./Score 2p./Composed: Feb. 1, 1947, to Mar. 29, 1947.

ADM 44 U-3. Animal Crackers. Unison song for children with piano accompaniment: Words by
   Frances McCollin

Children's Voices--unison, Pno. acc./Ms./Score 6p.

ADM 44 U-4. The Bathing Suit. Unison song for children with piano accompaniment. Words by
   Frances McCollin

Children's Voices--unison, Pno. acc./Ms./Score 4p./Completion date: June 24, 1936.

ADM 44 U-5. Bed Time. Words by Gelett H. Burgess

Children's Voices--unison, Pno. acc./Ms./Score 4p./Date of completion: Jan., 1922./First perf.:
Miss Traubel's Recital, Philadelphia, Pa., Dec. 22, 1933.

ADM 49 U-63. A Bird-Walk. Children's voices. Words by Frances McCollin

Children's Voices--unison, Pno. acc./Ms./Score 4p./First perf.: Miss Traubel's Recital, Philadelphia, Pa., Dec. 22, 1948.

ADM 44 U-6. Children's Day. Words by Frances McCollin

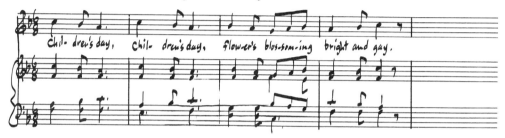

Children's Voices--unison, Pno. acc./Ms./Score 4p./Date of completion: Aug. 4, 1951./Arrangement for Children's voices four part: see ADM 51 F-1.

ADM 44 U-7. Christmas Shopping. Words by Frances McCollin

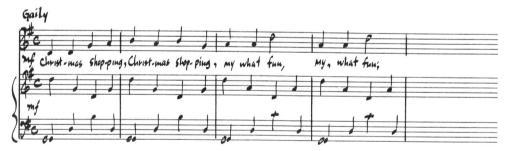

Children's Voices--unison, Pno. acc./Ms./Score 4p./Composed: Nov. 15, 1947.

ADM 44 U-8. Christmas Song. Words by Frances McCollin

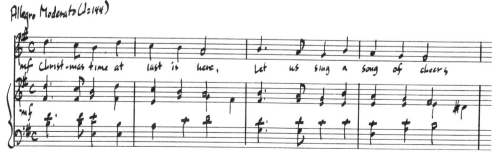

Children's Voices, Pno. acc./Ms./Score 6p./Composed: Dec. 5, 1933, to Dec. 13, 1933.

ADM 44 U-9.   Chocolate Buds.   Words by Frances McCollin

Children's Voices, unison, Pno. acc./Ms./Score 2p./Date of completion: July 4, 1939.

ADM 44 U-10.   Cream Puffs.   Unison song for children with piano accompaniment.   Words by
    Frances McCollin

Children's Voices, unison, Pno. acc./Ms./Score 2p./Possible completion date: June 26, 1936./
Pen name "Hancock" used.

ADM 44 U-11.   The Doll's Lullaby.   Words by Frances McCollin

Children's Voices, unison, Pno. acc./Ms./Score 6p./Date of completion: Nov. 29, 1933./First
perf.: Miss Traubel's Recital, Philadelphia, Pa., Dec. 29, 1948.

ADM 47 U-37. Eight Little Puppies. Unison song for children with piano accompaniment.
   Words by Frances McCollin

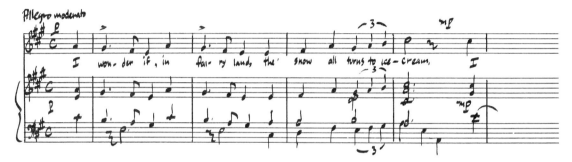

Children's Voices, unison, Pno. acc./Ms./Score 2p.

ADM 45 U-12. Fairy Food. Children's voices. Words by Frances McCollin

Children's Voices, unison, Pno. acc./Ms./Score 2p./Pen name "Hancock" used.

ADM 45 U-13. The Fur Coat Game. Children's voices. Words by Frances McCollin

Children's Voices, unison, Pno. acc./Ms./Score 4p.

ADM 45 U-14. Games. Children's voices. Words by Frances McCollin

Children's Voices, Pno. acc./Ms./Score 4p.

ADM 45 U-15. Going to the Park. Children's voices. Words by Frances McCollin

Children's Voices--unison, Pno. acc./Ms./Score 4p.

ADM 45 U-16. Going to the Zoo. Children's voices. Words by Frances McCollin

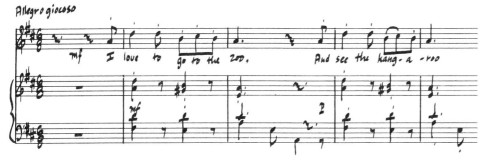

Children's Voices--unison, Pno. acc./Ms./Score 6p./First perf.: First Philadelphia All Girls' Chorus, Philadelphia, Pa., May 17, 1981.

ADM 45 U-17.   Good Night.   Children's voices.   Words by Frances McCollin

Children's Voices--unison, Pno. acc./Ms./Score 4p./First perf.:   Ethical Society, Philadelphia, Pa., Dec. 29, 1936.

ADM 49 U-60.   Grandma Grunts.   Words: North Carolina folk song

Children's Voices--unison, Pno. acc./Ms./Score 8p.

ADM 45 U-18.   Hop, Hop, Hippety Hop.   Children's voices.   Words by Frances McCollin

Children's Voices--unison, Pno. acc./Ms./Score 4p.

ADM 45 U-19.   The Hungry Cat.   Children's voices.   Words by Carolyn Wells

Children's Voices--unison, Pno. acc./Ms./Score 4p./First perf.:   Miss Traubel's Recital, Philadelphia, Pa., Dec. 27, 1933.

ADM 45 U-20. Ice Cream. Children's voices. Words by Frances McCollin

Children's Voices--unison, Pno. acc./Ms./Score 4p.

ADM 45 U-21. Ice Cream Cones. Children's voices. Words by Frances McCollin

Children's Voices--unison, Pno. acc./Ms./Score 4p./Pen name "Hancock" used.

ADM 45 U-22. If I Were the Toys. Children's voices. Words by Frances McCollin

Children's Voices--unison, Pno. acc./Ms./Score 4p.

ADM 45 U-61.   The June Song of the Wood Thrush.   Children's voices.   Words by Frances
   McCollin

Children's Voices--unison, Pno. acc./Ms./Score 2p./Date of completion: June 29, 1903./Same
music as "The Monkey Hand Organ." See ADM 46 U-27.

ADM 45 U-23.   Kittens.   Children's voices.   Words by Frances McCollin

Children's Voices--unison, Pno. acc./Ms./Score 4p.

ADM 45 U-24.   Little Orphan Annie.   Children's voices.   Words by Frances McCollin

Children's Voices--unison, Pno. acc./Ms./Score 10p./Date of completion: Oct. 19, 1948.

ADM 46 U-25.   May Day.   Words by Frances McCollin

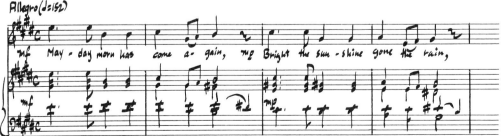
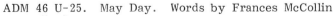

Children's Voices--unison, Pno. acc./Ms./Score 4p./Date of completion: Dec. 13, 1933./First
perf.: First Philadelphia All Girl's Chorus, Philadelphia, Pa., May 17, 1981.

ADM 46 U-26.   The Merry-Go-Round.   Words by Frances McCollin

Children's Voices--unison, Pno. acc./Ms./Score 2p./Date of completion: Apr. 10, 1948./Arrangement for children's voices, piano-four hands: see ADM 78 UD-2.

ADM 49 U-35A.   The Milkman.   See: Two Songs by Frances McCollin

ADM 46 U-27.   The Monkey Hand-organ.   Unison song for children with piano accompaniment.
   Words by Frances McCollin

Children's Voices--unison, Pno. acc./Ms./Score 8p./Date of completion: Sept. 8, 1935./Same
music as "The June Song of the Wood Thrush": see ADM 45 U-61.

ADM 46 U-28.   My Best Friend.   Unison children's song with piano accompaniment.   Words by
   Frances McCollin

Children's Voices--unison, Pno. acc./Ms./Score 4p./Date of completion: June 24, 1935.

ADM 46 U-29. My Pets. Unison song for children with piano accompaniment. Words by
    Frances McCollin

Children's Voices--Unison, Pno. acc./Ms./Score 4p./Date of completion: May 29, 1935.

ADM 46 U-30. New Year's Song. Words by Frances McCollin

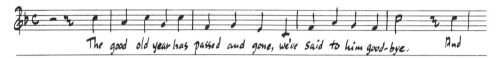

Children's Voices--unison, Pno. acc./Ms./Score 2p.

ADM 46 U-29. Now Dolly Dear. Unison children's song with piano accompaniment. Words by
    Frances McCollin

Children's Voices--unison, Pno. acc./Ms./Score 4p./Date of completion: June 16, 1935.

ADM 46 U-32. Off to the Woods. Words by Frances McCollin

Children's Voices--unison, Pno. acc./Ms./Score 2p.

ADM 46 U-33. On the Sand. Words by Frances McCollin

Children's Voices--unison, Pno. acc./Ms./Score 8p./Date of completion: Nov. 29, 1933.

ADM 46 U-34. Our Baby Sister. Words by Frances McCollin

Children's Voices--unison, Pno. acc./Ms./Score 2p. [3/4 size.]/Pen name "Hancock," used./
Same as "Our Little Baby" (see below).

ADM 46 U-34. Our Little Baby. Words by Frances McCollin

Children's Voices--unison, Pno. acc./Ms./Score 4p./Same as "Our Baby Sister."

ADM 47 U-35. Paper Dolls. Unison children's song with piano accompaniment. Words by
    Frances McCollin

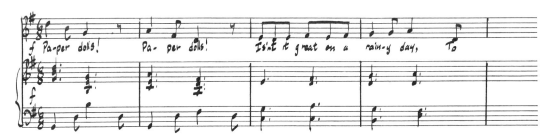

Children's Voices--unison, Pno. acc./Ms./Score 4p.

ADM 47 U-36.   Pleasant Pastimes.   Words by Frances McCollin

Children's Voices--unison, Pno. acc./Ms./Score 8p./Composed: Nov. 20, 1933-Nov. 29, 1933./
First perf.: Miss Traubel's Recital, Philadelphia, Pa., Dec. 29, 1948.

ADM 48 U-55B.   The Postman.   See: Two Songs by Frances McCollin

ADM 47 U-37.   The Purple Cat.   Words by Frances McCollin

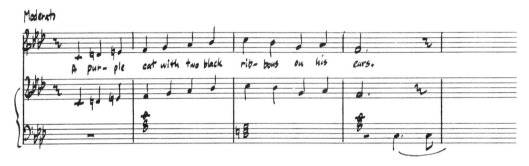

Children's Voices--unison, Pno. acc./Ms./Score 4p.

ADM 47 U-39.   A Rainy Day.   Unison song for children with piano accompaniment.   Words by
     Frances McCollin

Children's Voices--unison, Pno. acc./Ms./Score 4p.

ADM 47 U-40.   The Rope Swing.   Words by Frances McCollin

Children's Voices--unison, Pno. acc./Ms./Score 2p./Date of completion: Nov. 25, 1939./First perf.: Miss Traubel's Recital, Dec. 29, 1948.

ADM 47 U-41.   The Rubber Ball.   Unison song for children with piano accompaniment.   Words by Frances McCollin

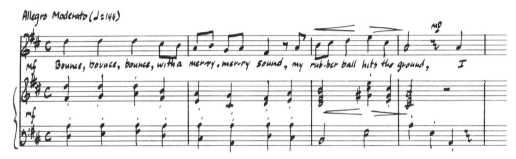

Children's Voices--unison, Pno. acc./Ms./Score 4p.

ADM 47 U-42.   Sandwiches.   Words by Frances McCollin

Children's Voices--unison, Pno. acc./Ms./Score 2p./Date of completion: July 9, 1941.

ADM 47 U-43.   Sandy.   Words by Frances McCollin

Children's Voices--unison, Pno. acc./Ms./Score 4p./Date of completion: Feb. 17, 1948.

ADM 47 U-46. The Seasons. Unison song for children with piano accompaniment. Words by Frances McCollin

Children's Voices--unison, Pno. acc./Ms./Score 10p./Date of completion: June 24, 1934.

ADM 48 U-47. Sister's Wedding. Unison song for children with piano accompaniment. Words by Frances McCollin

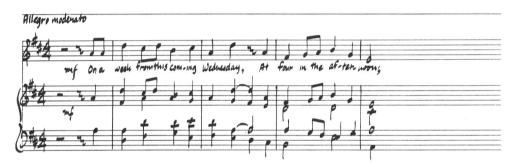

Children's Voices--Unison, Pno. acc./Ms./Score 4p./Date of completion: June 25, 1936.

ADM 48 U-48. South America. Words by Frances McCollin

Children's Voices--unison, Pno. acc./Ms./Score 4p./Date of completion: Aug. 3, 1943.

ADM 48 U-49. Spinach. Words by Frances McCollin

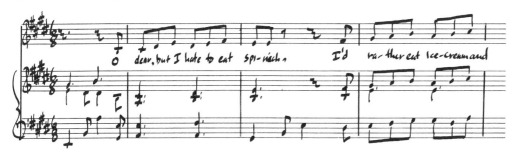

Children's Voices--unison, Pno. acc./Ms./Score 2p./Date of completion: Oct. 15, 1947.

ADM 48 U-50. Summer and Winter Days. Unison song for children with piano accompaniment.
  Words by Frances McCollin

Children's Voices--unison, Pno. acc./Ms./Score 4p.

ADM 48 U-51. Summer Showers. Unison song for children with piano accompaniment. Words
  by Frances McCollin

Children's Voices--unison, Pno. acc./Ms./Score 4p./Date of completion: June 30, 1935.

ADM 48 U-52. Swinging. Words by Frances McCollin

Children's Voices--unison, Pno. acc./Ms./Score 4p./Date of completion: Sept. 27, 1936.

ADM 48 U-53. Tinkle, Tinkle. Words by Frances McCollin

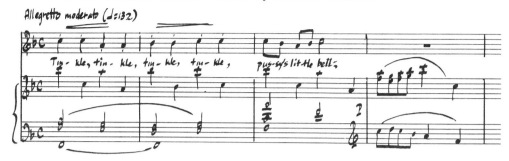

Children's Voices--unison, Pno. acc./Ms./Score 4p./Date of completion: Nov. 20, 1933.

ADM 48 U-54. Trains. Words by Frances McCollin

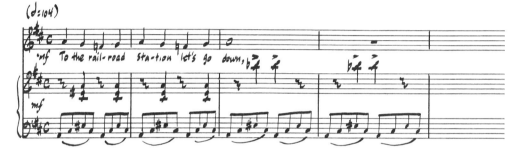

Children's Voices--unison, Pno. acc./Ms./Score 8p./Date of completion: July 26, 1943.

ADM 48 U-55A [Two songs by Frances McCollin]. The Milkman. Words by Frances McCollin

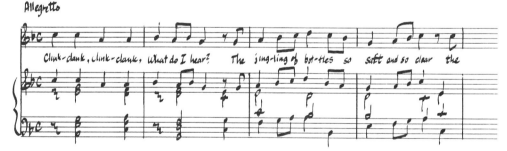

Children's Voices--unison, Pno. acc./Ms./Score 2p./Date of completion: Oct. 2, 1945./First
perf.: Miss Traubel's Recital, Philadelphia, Pa., Dec. 29, 1948.

ADM 48 U-55B [Two songs by Frances McCollin]. The Postman. Words by Frances McCollin

Children's Voices--unison, Pno. acc./Ms./Score 2p./Date of completion: Oct. 2, 1945.

ADM 48 U-56. What Does Little Birdie Say? Words by Frances McCollin

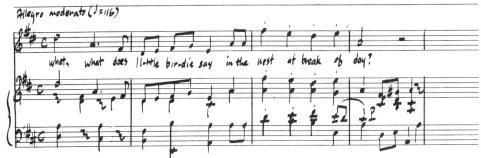

Children's Voices--unison, Pno. acc./Ms./Score 8p./Date of completion: Dec. 5, 1933.

ADM 48 U-57. Wildflowers. Words by Frances McCollin

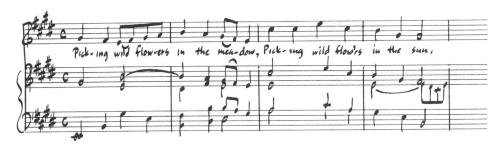

Children's Voices--unison, Pno. acc./Ms./Score 2p.

ADM 48 U-62. Windy Nights. Children's voices. Words by Frances McCollin

Children's Voices--unison, Pno. acc./Ms./Score 2p./Arrangement for children's voices: see
ADM 50 D-8.

ADM 49 U-58. Winter Mornings. Children's voices. Words by Frances McCollin

Children's Voices--unison, Pno. acc./Ms./Score 4p.

ADM 49 U-59. Winter Sports. Children's voices. Words by Frances McCollin

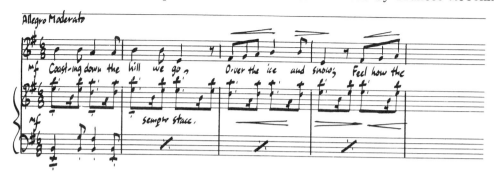

Children's Voices--unison, Pno. acc./Ms./Score 4p./First perf.: Miss Traubel's Recital, Philadelphia, Pa., Dec. 29, 1936.

VOCAL: CHILDREN'S VOICES--PIANO-FOUR HANDS

ADM 78 UD-1. August. Easy piano duet. Words by Frances McCollin

Children's Voices, Pno.-four hands/Ms./Score 2p.

ADM 78 UD-2. Letting the Old Cat Die. Words by Frances McCollin

Children's Voices, Pno.-four hands/Ms./Score 4p./Date of completion: May 12, 1937.

ADM 78 UD-3.   The Merry-Go Round.   Words by Frances McCollin

Children's Voices, Pno.-four hands/Ms./Score 4p.

ADM 78 UD-4.   Off to the Woods.   Unison song for children with piano accompaniment.   Words by Frances McCollin

Children's Voices, Pno.-four hands/Ms./Score 4p./Date of completion: Nov. 24, 1948 (on cover page).

ADM 78 UD-5.   Queen Alice.   Teaching piece.   Words by Frances McCollin

Children's Voices, Pno.-four hands/Ms./Score 10p./Part of song circle: see ADM 54 AW-2.

ADM 78 UD-6.   Saturday.   Duet.   Words by Frances McCollin

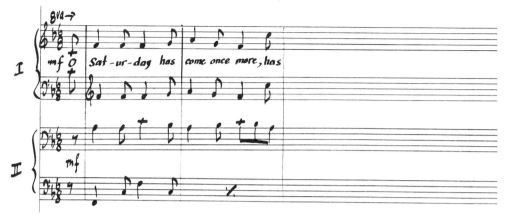

Children's Voices, Pno.-four hands/Ms./Score 4p./Composed: Feb. 4, 1949, to Feb. 9, 1949.

ADM 78 UD-7.   The Seashore Song.   Piano duet.   Words by Frances McCollin

Children's Voices, Pno.-four hands/Ms./Score 2p./Date of completion: Mar. 3, 1949.

ADM 78 UD-8.   Three Little Clover Blooms.   Words by Frances McCollin

Children's Voices, Pno.-four hands/Ms./Score 4p.

VOCAL: CHILDREN'S VOICES--DUET

ADM 50 D-1.   Canoeing.   Round for children's voices

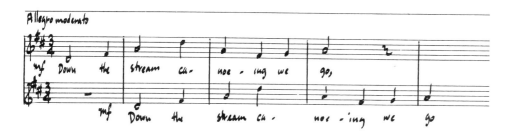

SA, Pno. acc./Ms./Score 2p./Date of completion: Sept. 8, 1936.

ADM 50 D-2.   The Cuckoo Clock.   Duet

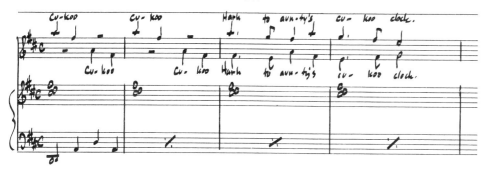

SA, Pno. acc./Ms./Score 4p./Date of completion: Sept. 12, 1948.

ADM 50 D-3.   Grasshopper Green.   Two-part children's chorus with piano accompaniment

SA, Pno. acc./Ms./Score 12p./Arrangement for women's voices: see ADM 73 LASS-5.

ADM 50 D-4.   In Winter I Get Up at Night.   Words by Robert Louis Stevenson

SA, Pno. acc./Ms./Score 4p./Composed: Sept. 29, 1940, to Oct. 27, 1940.

ADM 50 D-10.   Little Lamb Who Made Thee

SA, Org. acc./Ms./Score 6p.

ADM 50 D-5.   Pirate Story

SA, Pno. acc./Ms./Score 10p./Composed: Aug. 10, 1941, to Oct. 3, 1942.

ADM 50 D-6. Pussy Willow. Two-part chorus for children's voices with piano accompaniment.
Words: author unknown

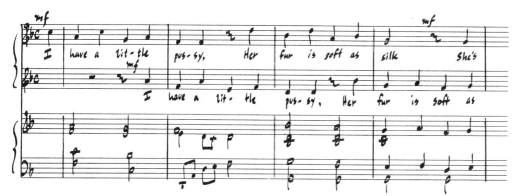

SA, Pno. acc./Ms./Score 8p.

ADM 50 D-9. Spring. Two-part chorus for children's voices with piano accompaniment. Words:
author unknown (3')

SA, Pno. acc./Mills Music © 1945./Score 10p./Dedicated to Frances Spector, supervisor of Music
Grade Schools, Camden, N.J./First perf.: Royer Greaves School Chorus, Philadelphia, Pa.,
June 23, 1951.

ADM 50 D-7. Swing Song. Words by Robert Louis Stevenson

SA, Pno. acc./Ms./Score 6p./Date of completion: Aug. 3, 1942.

ADM 50 D-8. Windy Nights.   Words by Robert Louis Stevenson

SA, Pno. acc./Ms./Score 4p./Date on score: Aug. 3, 1942.

VOCAL: CHILDREN'S VOICES--FOUR-PART

ADM 51 F-1. Children's Day. See: ADM 44 U-6. Children's Day

ADM 51 F-4. The Children's Friend. Hymn for children. Words by Frances McCollin

Children's Voices, Pno. acc./Ms./Score 4p./Arrangement for chorus: see ADM 59 H-6.

ADM 51 F-3. God Our Heavenly Father

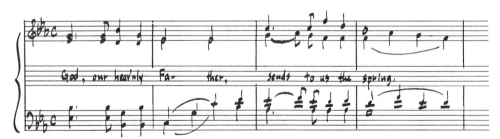

Children's Voices, Pno. acc./Ms./Score 2p./Date of completion: Aug. 14, 1939.

ADM 51 F-2. Jesus' Birthday. Children's hymn. Words by Frances McCollin

In the cold dark sta- ble,   on the prick-ly   hay.

Children's Voices, Pno. acc./Ms./Score 4p./Date of completion: Sept. 27, 1936./Dedicated to David Kirk Foster.

VOCAL: CHILDREN'S VOICES--CANTATA

ADM 52 UC-1. Pagliaccini. Words by Frances McCollin

Now, boys and   girls, come lis-ten to me.

Unison Voices, Pno. acc./Ms./Score 22p.

ADM 52 UC-2. 'Twas the Night Before Christmas (A Visit from St. Nicholas)

Twas the night be- fore Christ-mas, when all through the   house, not a

SA, Pno. acc./Arthur Schmidt Co., © 1923./Score 28p./Dedicated to Edward McCollin Arnett.

VOCAL: CHILDREN'S VOICES--MUSICAL PLAY

ADM 53 MP-1.   Goldilocks and the Three Bears.   Words by Frances McCollin

1.

2.

3.

4.

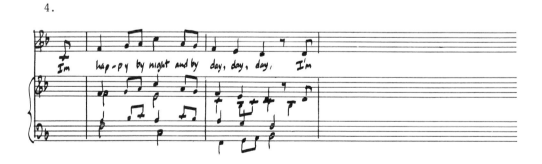

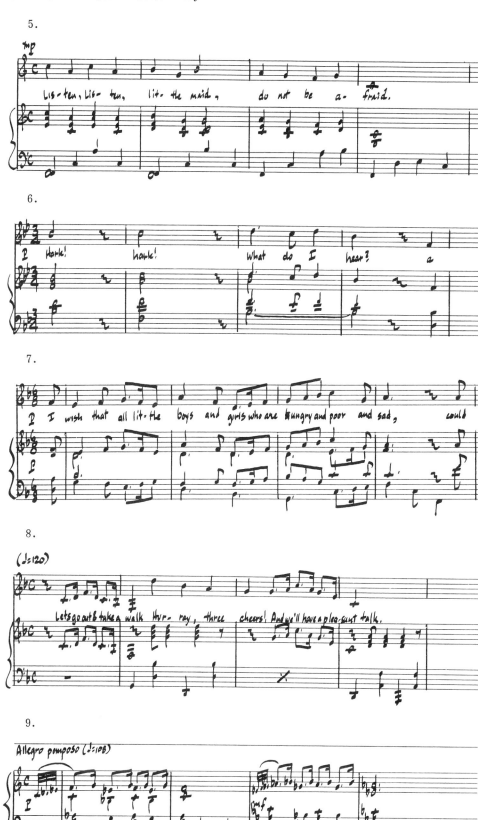

10.

11.

12.

13.

14.

15.

Oh! Oh what a cute lit-tle room with a cute lit-tle chair and a cute lit-tle ta-ble.

16.

Misterioso- Allegro non troppo

f Who's been sit-ting in my chair,

17.

Presto Agitato

f Look here! Look here! Some-one's been ly-ing on my bed!

18.

(♩=116)

Oh, mom-my and dad-dy come quick and see There's a great big doll on my bed,

19.

Allegro misterioso

Look, Look, she isn't a doll, She's a real lit-tle, true lit-tle, live lit-tle gir-lie,

20.

Children's Voices, Pno. acc./Ms./Score 76p./Dates various sections completed: 1. Granny and
Goldilocks: June 4, 1938; 2. Goldilocks Feeding Her Pets: July 16, 1938; 3. The Three Bears:
June 4, 1938; 4. Goldilocks Thoughts: July 8, 1939; 6. Goldilocks Reply: Aug. 14, 1938;
7. Wishing Song: Aug. 13, 1938; 8. Let's Go Out: Dec. 11, 1938; March of the Bears: July
17, 1938; 10. Up the Stream I Go: Nov. 13, 1938-Dec. 11, 1938; 11. The Discovery: Dec. 11,
1938; 12. Chair Song: Dec. 26, 1936; 14. Bedroom Song, Mar. 13, 1939-June 17, 1939; 15. Baby
Bear's Room: July 4, 1939; 17. Further Mysteries: Mar. 12, 1939; 18. Baby Bear's Surprise:
June 17, 1939-Dec. 18, 1939; 19. Goldilocks Asleep: Dec. 26, 1938-Mar. 12, 1939; 21. Reunion:
Dec. 18, 1939.

ADM 53 MP-2. Alice and the Calendar. Words by Frances McCollin

1.

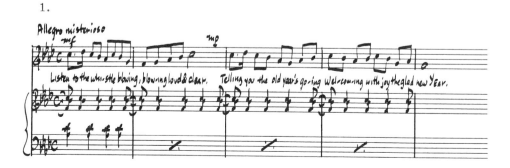

2.

Allegro moderato

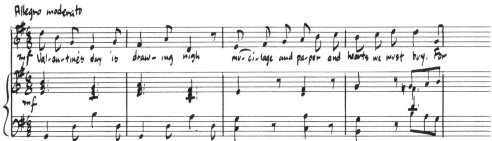

mf Val-en-tine's day is draw-ing nigh. mu-ci-lage and pa-per and hearts we must buy, For

3.

Strepitso

f March brings days when the wind blows high, It takes your hat right up to the sky. The

4.

Allegro giocoso

A - pril Fool! A - pril Fool! Cot-ton in your can - dy notes pinned on-to your dres-ses

5.

Allegro moderato

(*f*)

f Heigh-ho! For a pic - nic u - pon this love-ly day; For

6.

Andante Tranquillo

June, June, beau-ti-ful June, All the mea-dows are thick with po - sies.

12.

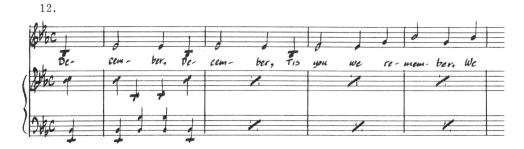

Children's Voices, Pno. acc./Ms./Score 80p.

VOCAL: CHILDREN'S VOICES--SONG CYCLE "ALICE IN WONDERLAND"

ADM 54 AW-2.   Alice in Wonderland, Queen Alice.   Words by Lewis Carroll

SATB, Pno. acc./Ms./Score 4p./Date of completion: Jan. 14, 1940./First perf.:   Gertrude Traubel, Philadelphia, Pa., Dec. 30, 1940.

ADM 54 AW-3.   Alice in Wonderland.   Beautiful Soup.   Words by Lewis Carroll

SATB, Pno. acc./Ms./Score 4p./Date of completion: Nov. 24, 1940.

ADM 54 AW-4.   Alice in Wonderland.   The Lion and the Unicorn.   Words by Lewis Carroll

SATB, Pno. acc./Ms./Score 2p./Date of completion: June 20, 1940.

ADM 54 AW-1. Alice in Wonderland. The Lobster Quadrille. Unison song for children with
piano accompaniment. Words by Lewis Carroll

SATB, Pno. acc./Ms./Score 8p./Composed Dec. 13, 1933, to June 14, 1934.

ADM 54 AW-5. Alice in Wonderland. Pig and Pepper. Words by Lewis Carroll

SATB, Pno. acc./Ms./Score 6p./Composed: Jan. 14, 1940, to May 11, 1940.

VOCAL: CHILDREN'S VOICES--OPERA

ADM 55 KC-1. King Christmas or King of the Holidays. Children's opera. Libretto by Charles
I. Junkin (20')

1.

3.

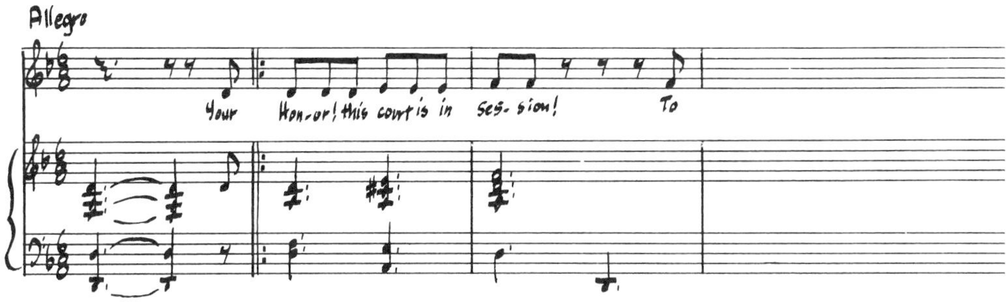
Allegro
Your Hon-or! this court is in ses- sion! To

4.

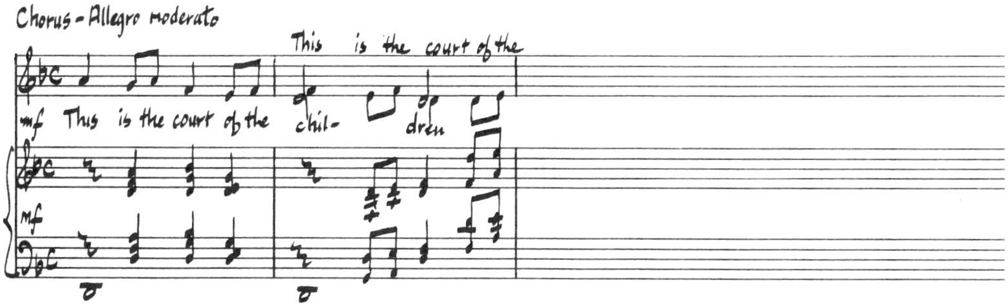
Chorus - Allegro moderato
This is the court of the
mf This is the court of the chil- dren
mf

5.

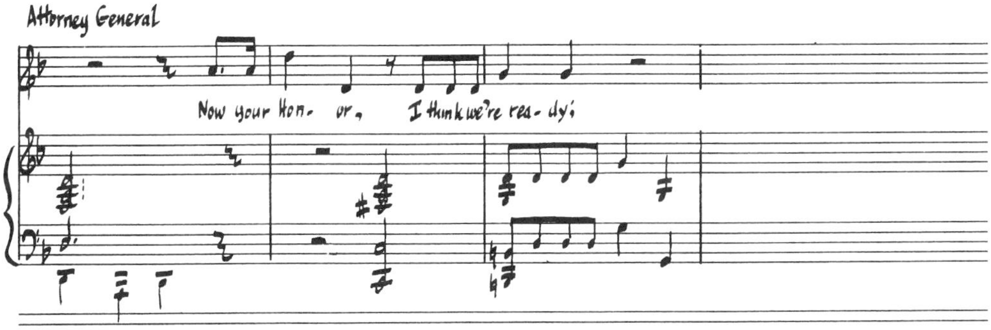
Attorney General
Now your Hon- or, I think we're rea- dy;

6.

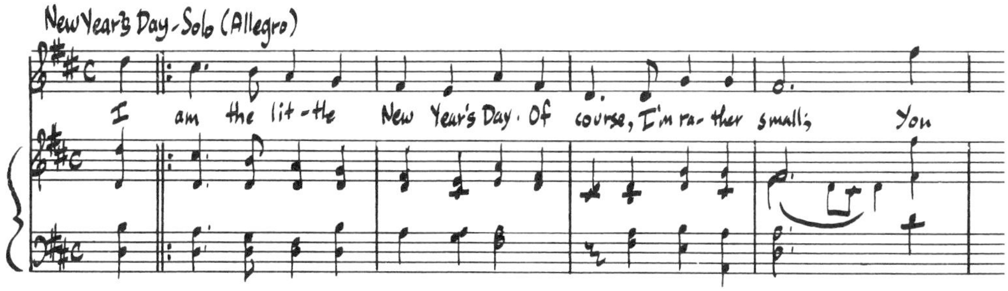
New Year's Day - Solo (Allegro)
I am the lit- tle New Year's Day. Of course, I'm ra- ther small; You

7.

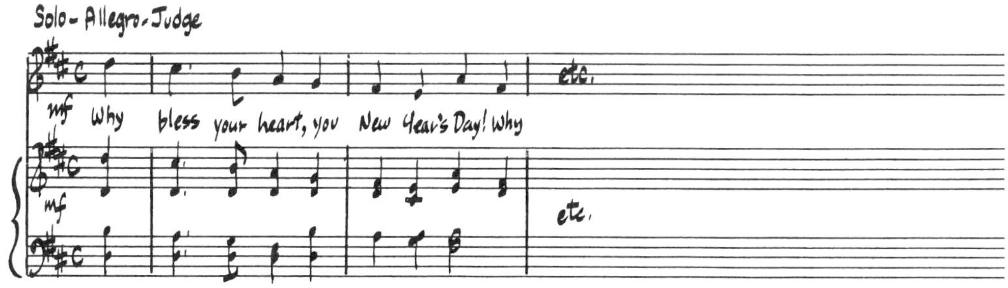
Solo - Allegro - Judge
etc.
mf Why bless your heart, you New Year's Day! Why
mf
etc.

8.

Larghetto - Valentine's Day

I am a Saint, St. Val-en-tine!

9.

Judge - Lento

Oh! sweet St. Val-en-tine, I quite a- gree! My

10.

Song of the Jury - moderato

O judge dear judge were feeling fun- ny!

O judge, dear judge were feeling fun- ny! We feel as emp-ty as a drum!

11.

Washington's Birthday - Solo

Most no- ble judge and la- dies fair And gent-le-men! I do de-clare I

12.

Judge - solo - moderato

Most hon- ored Claim-ant! Rest se- cure, Your

13.

14.

15.

16.

17.

18.

Allegro moderato-Judge

mf Now here is one of cu-ri-os mien! I

19.

Larghetto-Halloween

mf I'm Hal-low-een! When spooks are seen. And

20.

Judge-Allegro moderato

mf You're wel-come sir! You're just the sort To show us lots of merry sport!

21.

Larghetto-Thanksgiving Day

p My lit-tle friends, Your stir-ring song Will ling-er in my mem-ory long!

22.

Judge-Andante

mf Re-spect-ed friend, your words are true, Our debt is great, and rightly due.

23.

24.
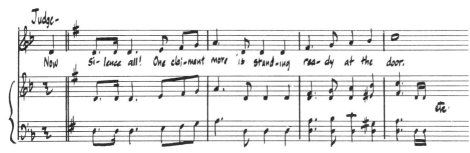

25.

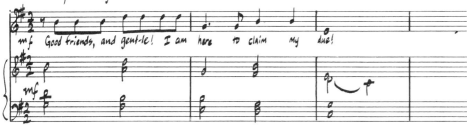

26.

27.

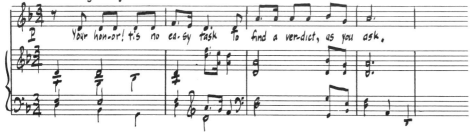

28.

29.

Children's Voices, Pno. acc./G. Schirmer, © 1926./Score 46p./Dedicated to cousin Edith Foster.

VOCAL: SOLO

*ADM 56 V-1. At Eventide. Words by James Arnold Blaisdell (3')

Solo voice, Pno. acc./H. W. Gray Co., © 1920./Score 6p./Dedicated to Edna Lewis./First perf.:
Philadelphia Music Club Chorus, Philadelphia, Pa., Jan. 27, 1920.

*ADM 57 V-16A.   Cycle of Three Songs for Low Voice from "In Memoriam."   Words by Alfred
    Tennyson

1. With Weary Steps I Loiter On

2. Wild Bird

3. Dear Friend, Far Off, My Lost Desire

Solo voice, Pno. acc./Ms./Score 12p./Date of completion: Aug. 25, 1921./Pen name "Alfred"
used./First perf.: Mary Bray, Philadelphia, Pa., Mar. 9, 1924.

ADM 57 V-16-C.   Dear Friend, Far Off, My Lost Desire.   See: Cycle of Three Songs for Low
    Voice

ADM 57 V-18.   An Evening Song.   Song for high voice.   Words by Sidney Lanier Lippincott

Solo voice, Pno. acc./Ms./Score 8p./Composed: May 7, 1937, to May 13, 1937./Submitted for W. W. Kimball Co., Prize of Chicago./Council of Teachers: July 1, 1937./Pen name "Mayfair" used.

ADM 56 V-2.   Fairest Lord Jesus

Solo voice, Org. acc./Ms./Score 8p./Composed: July 29, 1943, to Aug. 24, 1943.

ADM 56 V-3.   Into the Woods My Master Went.   Words by Sidney Lanier

Solo voice, Pno./Org, vn., hp. acc./J. Fischer and Bro., © 1940./Score 3p./Dedicated to Edward McCollin./First perf.: Collegiate Chorus of St. Nicholas Concert, New York, NY, Feb. 23, 1913.

ADM 56 V-4.   Invitation.   Words by Richard LeGallienne

Solo voice, Pno. acc./Ms./Score 8p./Pen name "Richard" and "Charles" used./First perf.:
Mary Bray, Philadelphia, Pa., Feb. 9, 1926.

ADM 56 V-5.   I Walked with You.   Words by Catherine Miller Balm

Solo voice, Pno. acc./Ms./Score 8p./Composed: Feb. 17, 1951, to Feb. 22, 1951./Dedicated to
J. Horace Balm./First perf.: Mary Maccarine, Philadelphia, Pa., May 21, 1951.

ADM 56 V-6.   The Lord is My Shepherd for Voice and Organ

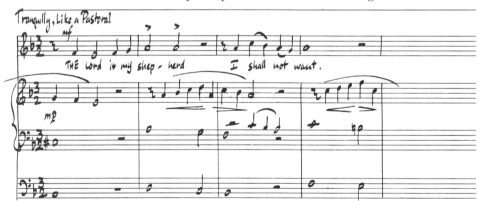

Solo voice, Org. acc./Ms./Score 8p./Pen name "Pastor" and "Shepherdson" used.

ADM 56 V-7. Love Took Me Softly by the Hand. Words: anonymous

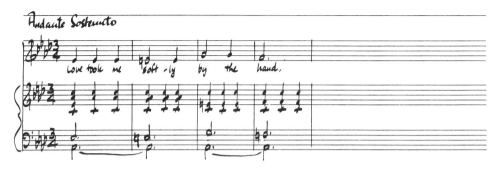

Solo voice, Pno. acc./Ms./Score 4p./Date of completion: May 1913./First perf.: Edward McCollin, Philadelphia, Pa., Jan. 5, 1915.

*ADM 56 V-8. The Midnight Sea. Words by John Hull Ingham

Solo voice, Pno. acc./Ms./Score 14p./Pen name "Graham" used./Awarded Class of 1919, National Federation of Music Clubs./No cover page. In ink./First perf.: Mrs. Leo Sach, Petersborough, NH, July 9, 1919.

*ADM 56 V-9. Pack Clouds Away. Words by Thomas Heywood

Solo voice, Pno. acc./Oliver Ditson Co., © 1942./Score 7p./Dedicated to Maria Koussevitzky./ First perf.: Mary Bray, Philadelphia, Pa., Feb. 9, 1926.

*ADM 56 V-10.   Robin, Little Robin.   Song with pianoforte accompaniment.   Words: anonymous

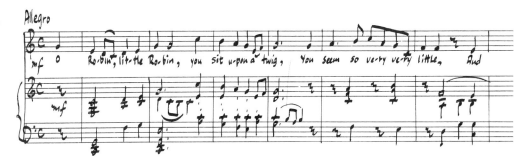

Solo voice, Pno. acc./Arthur Schmidt Co., © 1919, © 1922./Score 6p./Dedicated to and sung by Frieda Hempel./Arrangement for women's voices: see ADM 94 LASS-15./First perf.:   Kitty McCollin, Philadelphia, Pa., Nov. 26, 1918.

ADM 57 V-17.   Serenade

Solo voice, Pno. acc./Ms./Score 4p./Composed Aug. 24, 1943, to Aug. 31, 1943.

*ADM 57 V-11.   Sleep Holy Babe.   Words by E. Caswell

Solo voice, Pno. acc./Oliver Ditson Co., © 1930./Score 8p./Dedicated to Luba Stokowska[y]./ First perf.:   Dyan Fitts, Philadelphia, Pa., Nov. 11, 1928.

ADM 57 V-15. Song at Midnight. Words by Catherine Balm

Solo voice, Pno. acc./Ms./Score 6p./Date of completion: Feb. 26, 1951./First perf.: Mary Maccarine, Philadelphia, Pa., May 21, 1951.

ADM 57 V-12. The Things of Everyday Are All So Sweet. Words by Alice Allen (3')

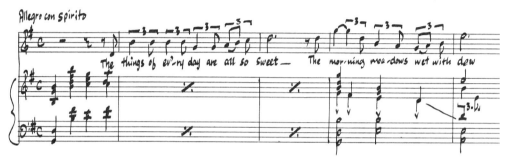

Solo voice, Pno. acc./Arthur Schmidt Co., © 1923./First perf.: Kitty McCollin, Philadelphia, Pa., Nov. 26, 1918.

ADM 57 V-13. Thou Art Like unto a Flower

Solo voice, Pno. acc./Ms./Score 4p./Date of completion: May 1910./First perf.: Edward McCollin, Philadelphia, Pa.. May 18, 1911.

ADM 57 V-16 B. Wild Bird. See: Cycle of Three Songs for Low Voice

*†ADM 57 V-19. Winds of God. Words by Clinton Sealeard

Solo voice, Pno. acc./Ms./Score 24p./Date of completion: Dec. 1915./Awarded 1918 prize by Philadelphia Society of Arts and Letters./First perf.: Society of Arts and Letters, Philadelphia, Pa., Apr. 17, 1918.

ADM 57 V-16A. With Weary Steps I Loiter On. See: Cycle of Three Songs for Low Voice

VOCAL: SACRED CHORAL, A CAPPELLA

ADM 59 H-11. All My Heart This Night Rejoices. Christmas anthem for mixed voices (a cappella). Words by Paulus Gerhardt (4')

SATB/T. Fischer and Bros., © 1943./Score 8p./Dedicated to Miss Kathryn R. O'Boyle./Part of Morningside College Choir Series./Selected and edited by Paul MacCollin./Tr. by Catherine Winkworth (1858).

ADM 59 H-2. Almighty Father, Who Dost Give (Hymn 207)

SATB/Ms./Score 2p.

ADM 59 H-3.   The Beatitudes.   Words: St. Matthew 4.24 to 5.16

SATB/Ms./Score 20p./Date of completion: Dec. 1, 1949.

ADM 59 H-4.   Behold the Lamb of God.   Words by Frances McCollin

SATB/Ms./Score 2p./Pen name "Mayfair" used.

ADM 59 H-5.   Calm on the Listening Ear of Night.   Carol-anthem for mixed voices, unaccompanied.   Words by Edmund Sears (4')

SATB/The H. W. Gray Co., © 1928./Score 8p./Dedicated to the A Cappella Choir of Philadelphia, Harold W. Gilbert, Conductor./First perf.: A Cappella Choir of Philadelphia, Pa., Feb. 26, 1929.

ADM 59 H-6.   The Children's Friend.   Words by Frances McCollin

SATB/Ms./Score 8p./Composed: Sept. 19, 1942-Sept. 26, 1942.

ADM 59 H-7. Christmas Lullaby. Words by Frances McCollin

SATB/Theodore Presser, © 1938./Score 5p./Dedicated to Roma Angel and the Choir of St. Matthew's P.E. Church, Philadelphia./Arrangement for women's voices: see ADM 71 WW-1./ First perf.: St. Stephen's Church, Philadelphia, Pa., Dec. 19, 1937.

*ADM 59 H-8. Come Hither, Ye Faithful. Christmas carol-anthem for mixed voices (six-part) by E. Caswall from Adeste Fideles (4')

SATB, Sop. solo, Ten. solo./Oliver Ditson Co., © 1927./Score 10p./Second prize: donated by Mrs. H. E. Talbott for a sacred composition--used by the Westminster Choir, Dayton, Ohio, 1926./Arrangement for women's voices: see ADM WW-2./First perf.: Westminster Choir, Westminster, NJ, Nov. 29, 1927.

ADM 59 H-9. Dear Lord and Father of Mankind. Anthem for chorus of mixed voices. Words by John Greenleaf Whittier (5')

SATB/Galaxy Music Corp., © 1938./Score 11p./Dedicated to Paul MacCollin and the Choir of Morningside College, Sioux City, Iowa.

ADM 59 H-10.   Dream of the Christ Child.   Sacred madrigal for eight-part mixed chorus.   Words by Kate Ward

SSAATTBB /St. Mary's Press, © 1957./Score 19p./Dedicated to Angeline Christaldi and the Bartram High School Concert Choir./Based on hymn Fairest Lord Jesus.   See ADM 56 V-2./ First perf.:   John Bartram High School Chorus, Philadelphia, Pa., Dec. 12, 1930.

ADM 59 H-11.   Eternal God, Whose Power Upholds.   Words by Frances McCollin

SATB /Ms./Score 4p.

ADM 60 H-12.   For All the Saints.   Anthem for All Saint's Day.   Words by William Walsham How

SATB /Ms./Score 22p./Composed: Nov. 8, 1948 to Mar. 19, 1949.

ADM 60 H-13.   Hail to the King of Glory.   Christmas anthem for eight-part mixed chorus.   Words by Christina G. Rossetti   (4')

SSAATTBB /H. W. Gray Co., © 1937./Score 11p./Dedicated to Henry S. Fray, conductor, and the Choral Club of the Musical Art Society, Camden, NJ./First perf.:   Camden Music Arts Society, Camden, NJ, Dec. 21, 1937.

*ADM 60 H-14. He Is Risen. Easter carol (4')

SATB/The H. W. Gray Co., © 1919./Score 10p./In Memoriam: Maude Sproule./First perf.:
Church of St. Luke and the Epiphany, Philadelphia, Pa., Apr. 16, 1919.

ADM 60 H-15. The Holy Birth. From "The True God," a choral cycle of the life of Christ.
   Christmas anthem for eight-part mixed chorus. Words by Harriet McEwen Kimball (4')

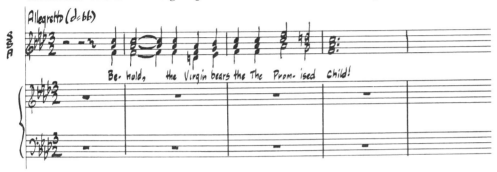

SSAATTBB/Oliver Ditson, © 1930./Score 12p./Dedicated to David McKay Williams and the Choir
of Bartholomew's Church, New York./First perf.: Montreat Adult Choir, Summa Music Festival,
Montreat, N.C., Aug. 21, 1937.

ADM 60 H-16. Hymn for the Y. Words by Frances McCollin

SATB/Ms./Score 4p./Entered in Centennial Hymn Contest: Jan. 4, 1954.

ADM 59 H-2. Hymn 207. See: Almighty Father, Who Dost Give

ADM 59 H-4. Hymn 280. See: Behold the Lamb of God

ADM 63 H-43. Hymn 331

SATB/Ms./Score 1p./Date of completion: Oct. 11, 1906./Christmas present to father, Edward McCollin: Dec. 25, 1906.

ADM 63 H-41. Hymn 457

SATB/Ms./Score 1p./Birthday present for Edward McCollin: July 6, 1906.

ADM 60 H-17. Hymn S-461

SATB/Ms./Score 2p./Pen name "Mayfair" used.

ADM 60 H-18. Hymn S-462

SATB/Ms./Score 2p./Pen name "Mayfair" used by Frances McCollin.

ADM 60 H-19. Hymn S-463

SATB/Ms./Score 2p./Pen name "Mayfair" used.

ADM 61 H-26. Hymn 506. See: Praise My Soul the King of Heaven

ADM 63 H-42. Hymn 584

SATB/Ms./Score 1p./Date of completion: Aug. 24, 1906.

ADM 62 H-40. Hymn 612. Words: St. Paul

SATB/Ms./Score 1p./Dedicated to Miss Sproule.

ADM 72 H-45. Hymn Tunes

SATB/Ms./Score 2p./In the handwriting of Edward G. McCollin.

ADM 62 H-39. Kyrie

SATB/Ms./Score 1p./Date of completion: Dec. 17, 1907./Christmas gift for father, Edward G. McCollin.

ADM 62 H-37.   Laus Deo.   Words by Frank Dempster Sherman

SATB/Ms./Score 1p./Date of completion: Dec. 14, 1908.

ADM 60 H-20.   My Peace I Leave with You.   Eight-part anthem for mixed voices.   Words by
    Helen A. Dickinson

SSAATTBB/Oliver Ditson Co., © 1926./Score 10p./Dedicated to Harold W. Gilbert, conductor,
and the choir of St. Peter's Protestant Episcopal Church, Philadelphia./First perf.: Brahms
Chorus, Philadelphia, Pa., Jan. 19, 1927.

†ADM 61 H-21.   Now the Day Is Over.   Mixed voices, unaccompanied.   Words by S. Baring-
    Gould   (5')

SATB/The H. W. Gray Co., © 1926./Score 10p./Dedicated to Herbert J. Tiley, Mus. Doc., composer of the "Good Night" chime of radio station WFI, Philadelphia, which is used as the theme
of this composition./Prize: Strawbridge and Clothier, 1925.

ADM 62 H-35.   O Come and Mourn.   Anthem for mixed voices, a cappella.   Words by Frederick
    W. Faber

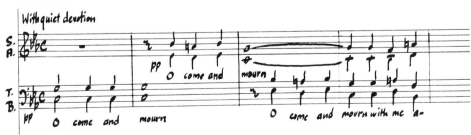

SATB/Oliver Ditson Co., © 1953./Score 9p./Dedicated to Edward McCollin Arnett./First perf.:
Arch Church Presbyterian, Philadelphia, Pa., Apr. 12, 1963.

ADM 61 H-22. O Love That Will Not Let Me Go (6')

SATB/Ms./Score 2p./Composed: Apr. 5, 1948, to Apr. 4, 1949.

ADM 61 H-23. "O Master Let Me Walk with Thee." Four-part a cappella. Words by Washington
Gladden

SATB/Ms./Score 18p./Composed: June 28, 1952, to June 30, 1953./Pen name "Burton" used./
Dedicated to Philadelphia Symphony Chorale, Oscar Eurmann, Conductor.

*ADM 79 H-24. Owe No Man Anything, Save to Love One Another. Offertory anthem for four-
part mixed chorus. Words: Romans xiii:8 (3')

SATB/E. Schirmer Inc., © 1919./Score 7p./First perf.: Church of the Holy Trinity, Philadelphia,
Pa., Oct. 19, 1919.

†ADM 61 H-25. Peace I Leave with You. Anthem for mixed voices. Words: St. John 14:27,
16:33 (4')

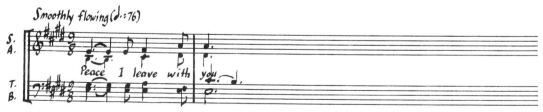

SATB/Carl Fischer Inc., © 1942./Score 6p./Dedicated to Merritt Eugene Garst, Jr./Prize:
Capital University, Ohio, 1941./First perf.: Chapel Choir of Capital University, Columbus, Ohio,
Apr. 19, 1941.

ADM 61 H-26. Praise My Soul the King of Heaven

SATB/Ms./Score 1p./Pen name "Mayfair" used.

ADM 65 HA-17. A Prayer. Anthem for mixed voices a cappella (3')

SSAATTBB/Carl Fischer Inc., © 1934./Score 5p./Dedicated to John Finley Williamson Westminster Choir School, Princeton, N.J./First perf.: First Presbyterian Church, Philadelphia, Pa., Oct. 22, 1961.

ADM 62 H-38. A Processional Hymn

SATB/Ms./Score 1p./Hymn for wedding anniversary of mother and father.

ADM 61 H-28. The Quest of Mary. Words by Edward W. Evans

SATB/Ms./Score 16p./Date of completion: July 29, 1943.

ADM 61 H-29. Rejoice, the Lord Is King

SATB/Ms./Score 1p./Pen name "Mayfair" used.

ADM 61 H-30. Resurrection from "The True God: A Choral Cycle on the Life of Christ." For
    eight-part chorus a cappella. Words by Elia W. Peattie (5')

SSAATTBB/Oliver Ditson Co., © 1927./Score 11p./Dedicated to the Brahms Chorus, Philadelphia,
N. Lindsay Norden, conductor./First perf.: Philadelphia Music Club, Philadelphia, Pa., Apr. 30,
1927.

*ADM 62 H-36. The Shepherds Had an Angel. Words by Christina Rosetti

SATB/Ms./Score 19p./Arrangement for women's voices: see ADM 70 WS-1./Piece awarded first
prize in the competitions of Sigma Alpha Iota 1938 (women's voices).

ADM 62 H-31. Shouting Sun. Spiritual. Words by Nancy Byrd Turner (3')

SAATB/Theodore Presser Co., © 1934./Score 9p./Dedicated to Hall Johnson./First perf.:
Musical Arts Society Choral, Camden, N.J., May 22, 1934.

ADM 62 H-32.   Sing Alleluia!   An eight-part carol for mixed voices, solo tenor, baritone, and bass.   Unaccompanied   (4')

SSAATTBB/G. Schirmer Inc., © 1934./Score 9p./Dedicated to Harold Gleason./First perf.: Fifth Avenue Presbyterian Church, New York, NY, Dec. 25, 1934.

*†ADM 62 H-33.   Then Shall the Righteous Shine.   Unaccompanied anthem in eight parts   (5')

SSAATTBB/The H. W. Gray Co., © 1921./Score 16p./Prize: Mendelssohn Club, 1920./First perf.: Mendelssohn Club, Philadelphia, Pa., Apr. 20, 1921.

ADM 62 H-34.   The Way of the Cross.   From "The True God: A Choral Cycle in the Life of Christ."   For eight-part chorus (with alto solo) a cappella.   Words by Henry H. Bonnell (7')

SATB/Oliver Ditson Co., © 1928./Score 12p./Dedicated to Dr. Healey Willan.

VOCAL: SACRED CHORAL, ACCOMPANIED

ADM 65 HA-12.   Agnus Dei.   See: O Lamb of God

ADM 64 HA-1.   Awake, My Soul

SATB, Org. acc./Ms./Score 2p./No words on score.   From the hymn of the same name.

ADM 64 HA-2.   Behold the Works of the Lord

SATB, Org. acc./Ms./Score 32p./Composed: Aug. 3, 1942, to Oct. 3, 1942./Words from the
Bible./Pen name "Awbury" used.

ADM 64 HA-3.   Come, My Soul, Thou Must Be Waking

SATB, Org. acc./Ms./Score 2p./No words.   Refer to hymn of same title.

ADM 64 HA-4. The Cross Was His Own. Anthem for Good Friday. Words: anonymous

SATB, Org./Pno. acc./Ms./Score 8p.

ADM 64 HA-5. Dedication

SATB, Org. acc./Ms./Score 8p./Composed: June 30, 1953-Aug. 3, 1953.

*†ADM 66 HA-26.   Fantasia on "O Little Town of Bethlehem." Words by Phillips Brooks (5')

SATB, Pno./Org. acc./Boosey and Hawkes, © 1948./Score 15p./Dedicated to Herbert Stavely
Sammond and the Choir of the Middle Collegiate Church, New York City./Opening theme: traditional English carol, Herefordshire, "The Truth Sent from Above."/Prize: Harvey Gaul Contest, 1947. Copyright 1948 in USA by Boosey and Hawkes Inc. All rights reserved. Copyright for all countries. Printed in USA. Boosey and Hawkes 16465.

ADM 65 HA-30.   Festival Chorus.   See: Ring Out Wild Bells

*ADM 64 HA-6.   God Is Our Refuge and Strength

SATB, Org. acc./The Arthur P. Schmidt Co., © 1922./Score 10p./First perf.: Church of
Divine Paternity, New York, NY, Sept. 24, 1922.

ADM 66 HA-27.   God So Loved the World.   Words: John III v. 16 (3')

SATB, Pno. acc./T. Presser Co., © 1914./Score 4p./First perf.: Overbrook Presbyterian
Church, Overbrook, Pa., Apr. 29, 1917.

ADM 64 HA-7. How Living Are the Dead!   Chorus for mixed voices, harp and organ.   Words by
   Florence Earle Coates (3')

SATB, Org., Hp. acc./Oliver Ditson Co., © 1944./Score 17p./Dedicated to David McK. Williams./
An acc. for pno.-4 hands available./First perf.: St. Bartholomew Church, Philadelphia, Pa.,
Nov. 5, 1944.

*ADM 65 HA-11.   Jubilate Deo in A (O Be Joyful in the Lord).   Mixed voices.   Words: Psalm C
   (3')

SATB, Org., acc./Oliver Ditson Co., © 1916./Score 8p./First perf.: St. Paul's Church,
Cheltenham, Pa., Jan. 24, 1915.

*†ADM 64 HA-8.   The Lord Is King.   Anthem for four voices   (4')

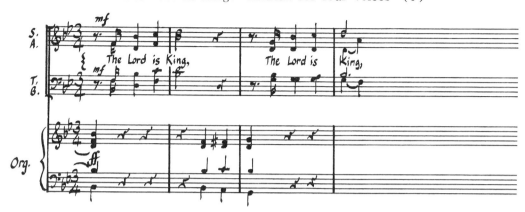

SATB, Org. acc./The H. W. Gray Co., © 1918./Score 14p./Prize: The Clemson Gold Medal,
American Guild of Organists, 1918./First perf.: Calvary Methodist Church, Philadelphia, Pa.,
Nov. 10, 1918.

*ADM 64 HA-9.   Mass for the Feast of St. Mark.   Four-part setting for mixed voices

  1. Kyrie

  2. Gloria

3. Sanctus

4. Agnus Dei

SATB, Org. Acc./The H. W. Gray Co., © 1918./Score 14p./Prize: The Clemson Gold Medal,
American Guild of Organists, 1918.

ADM 79 HA-10.   A New Commandment Give I Unto You.   Anthem for four voices   (3')

SATB, Org. acc./Oliver Ditson Co., © 1921./Score 5p./Date of completion: August 1916./
First perf.:   St. Stephen's Church, Philadelphia, Pa., Oct. 28, 1928.

ADM 66 HA-25. Nunc Dimittis

SATB, Org. acc./Ms./Score 2p./Transcribed by Edward McCollin

ADM 65 HA-11. O Be Joyful in the Lord. See: Jubilate Deo

ADM 65 HA-12. O! Lamb of God. Agnus Dei (3')

SATB, Org. acc./Theodore Presser, © 1907./Score 2p./First perf.: Calvary Methodist Episcopal
Church, Philadelphia, Pa., Feb. 23, 1908.

ADM 66 HA-26. O Little Town of Bethlehem. Fantasia. See: Fantasia on "O Little Town of
    Bethlehem."

*†ADM 79 HA-13. O Sing unto the Lord a New Song. Words: Psalm 96:1.3.11.12.13

SATB, Org. acc./The Boston Music Co., © 1921./Score 9p./Date of completion: January 1916./
Award: Manuscript Music Society, 1916./First perf.: Manuscript Music Society, Philadelphia,
Pa., Dec. 13, 1916./Used by permission of the publisher, The Boston Music Co., 116 Boylston
St., Boston, MA 02116.

ADM 65 HA-14.   O Day of Rest and Gladness

SATB, Org. acc./Ms./Score 2p.

ADM 65 HA-15.   O Give Thanks unto the Lord

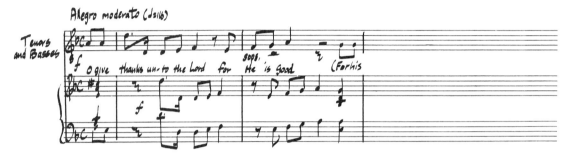

SATB, Pno. acc./Ms./Score 20p./Composed: March 16, 1939, to Aug. 25, 1939.

ADM 65 HA-16.   Once to Every Man and Nation.   Words by Lowell

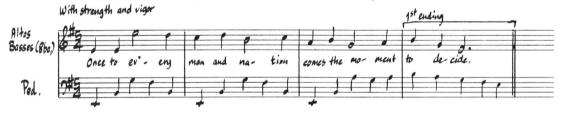

SATB, Org. acc./Ms./Score 8p.

ADM 65 HA-18. Prophecy. Words: Micah 4, Isaiah and Psalms

SATB, Pno. acc./Ms./Score 14p./Composed: June 14, 1944 (incomplete)./Pen name "Micah"
and "Ernest" used./Submitted in AGO Anthem Contest 1952-1953.

ADM 65 HA-19. Ring Out Wild Bells. Mixed chorus with orchestral accompaniment. Words by
    Alfred Tennyson (5')

SATB, Orchestral acc.: 2 Fl., 2 Ob., 2 Cl., 2 Bn.-2Hn., 2 Tpt., 1 Tbn./Elkan Vogel Co.,
© 1948./Score 21p./Composed: July 25, 1937, to June 7, 1938./Dedicated to Elsie Mecaskie,
conductor, High School Chorus, Atlantic City, N.J./First perf.: Philadelphia Bach Festival
Society, Philadelphia, Pa., Mar. 7, 1949.

ADM 66 HA-21. Te Deum [Laudamus]

SATB, Org. acc./Ms./Score 18p./Date of completion: July 17, 1950./First perf.: St. Stephen's
Church, Philadelphia, Pa., May 28, 1916.

ADM 66 HA-23. Welcome Happy Morning. Words by Venantius Fortunatus

SATB, Org. acc./Lawson-Gould, G. Schirmer, Inc., © 1967./Score 16p./Composed: Dec. 3, 1939, to May 26, 1940./John Ellerton, 1868, tr. of poet's text.

ADM 66 HA-25. Ye Watchers and Ye Holy Ones. Anthem SSAATB with organ accompaniment.
    Words by Athelstan Riley

SATB, org. acc./C. C. Birchard & Co., © 1940./Score 9p./Dedicated to Dr. Alexander McCurdy and the Choir of the Second Presbyterian Church of Philadelphia./First perf.: Second Presbyterian Church, Philadelphia, Pa., Feb. 23, 1941.

VOCAL: SACRED CHORAL, CANTATA, ACCOMPANIED

ADM 67 FIN-1. How Firm a Foundation. Words: Welsh Air-St. Denis

1.

2.

With calm assurance (♩=96)

Unison Chorus

mf How firm a foun-da-tion, ye saints of the Lord,

Org.

Ped

3.

Tranquillo ♩=116

man.

Ped.

4.

With restless Agitation ♩=160

man.

ped.

5.

Fast and Furiously ♩=126

man.

ped.

6.

SATB, Org. acc./Ms./Score 36p./Completion of various sections: I. How Firm a Foundation--Apr. 26, 1941. II. Fear Not, I Am with You--June 1, 1941-June 12, 1941. III. When Through the Deep Waters--June 12, 1941-June 30, 1941. IV. When Through Fiery Trials--June 8, 1941-July 9, 1941./First perf.: First Baptist Church, Philadelphia, Pa., Jan. 11, 1943.

VOCAL: SECULAR CHORAL, A CAPPELLA

ADM 68 SUM-1. Come Live with Me and Be My Love. Words by Christopher Marlowe

SATB/Boosey and Hawkes, © 1961./Score 14p./First perf.: Drexel Music Festival, Philadelphia, Pa., May 3, 1969.

ADM 68 SUM-3. A May Madrigal. Words by Henrietta Jewett Keith

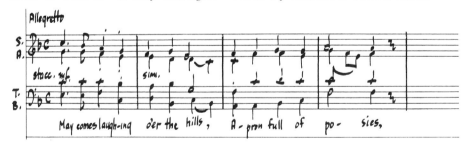

SATB/The Arthur P. Schmidt Co., © 1926./Score 6p./First perf.: Fireside Quartet, Philadelphia, Pa., May 1, 1929.

*†ADM 68 SUM-4.   The Nights O' Spring.   A Madrigal for mixed voices.   Words by Bertha
   Ochsner

SSATB/Oliver Ditson Co., © 1919./Score 12p./Awarded the W. W. Kimball Company Prize,
offered by the Chicago Madrigal Club in 1918./First perf.: Mendelssohn Club, Philadelphia,
Pa., Feb. 26, 1919.

ADM 68 SUM-5.   The Pixy People.   Words by James Whitcomb Riley   (7')

SATB/G. Schirmer, Inc., © 1942./Score 24p./Dedicated to Ralph L. Baldwin.

ADM 68 SUM-6.   A Roundelay.   Words by A. J. Perman, M.A.   (4')

SATB/Oliver Ditson Co., © 1925./Score 11p./First perf.: Institute for Instruction of the Blind
Recital, Philadelphia, Pa., May 21, 1925.

ADM 68 SUM-11.   Royer Greaves School Song.   Words by Frances McCollin

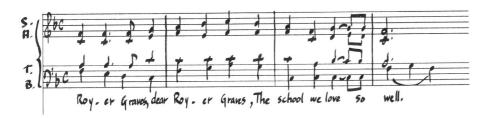

SATB/Ms./Score 4p./Date of completion: Feb. 5, 1951.

ADM 68 SUM-7. A Song of Spring. Madrigal for eight-part mixed chorus, a cappella. Words
by John Hall Ingham (5')

SSAATTBB/Oliver Ditson, © 1934./Score 17p./Dedicated to Fabien Sevitzky.

ADM 68 SUM-8. A Song of the Four Seasons. Madrigal for chorus of mixed voices. Words
by Austin Dobson (5')

SATB/G. Schirmer, © 1924./Score 11p./Dedicated to the Chicago Madrigal Club, D. A. Clip-
pinger, conductor./First perf.: Chicago Madrigal Club, Chicago, Ill., March 25, 1926.

ADM 68 SUM-9. The Spirit of Spring. Unaccompanied chorus for mixed voices in eight parts.
Words by Cora Fabbri (5')

SSAATTBB/Ms./Score 16p.

*†ADM 68 SUM-10.   What Care I? Madrigal for chorus of mixed voices.   Words by George
    Wither   (4')

SATB/Oliver Ditson Co., © 1923./Score 14p./Awarded the W. W. Kimball Prize, offered by the
Chicago Madrigal Club, 1923./First perf.: Philadelphia Music Club, Philadelphia, Pa., Jan. 27,
1925.

VOCAL: SECULAR CHORAL, ACCOMPANIED

ADM 69 SAC-1.   Ann Hutchinson's Exile. Words by Edward Everett Hale

SATB, S. and Bar. solo, Pno. acc. (Vn. obligato)/Ms./Score 32p./Composed: July 7, 1949,
to Sept. 20, 1949./Pen name "Pilgrim" used.

*ADM 69 SAC-2. Snow Flakes. Part song for mixed voices with words by Mary Mapes Dodge

Ms./Score 8p./Arrangement for women's voices: see ADM 74 LASS-17./First perf.: Manuscript
Music Society, Philadelphia, Pa., Nov. 25, 1919.

VOCAL: SACRED CHORAL--WOMEN'S VOICES, A CAPPELLA

*†ADM 70 WS-1. A Christmas Carol [The Shepherds Had an Angel]. Women's voices. Words
by Christina G. Rossetti

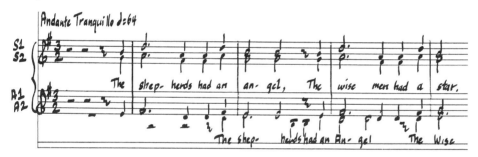

SSAA/Ms./Score 12p./Date of completion: Nov. 28, 1937./Prize: Sigma Alpha Iota, 1938.

ADM 70 WS-1. The Shepherds Had an Angel. See: A Christmas Carol. [The Shepherds Had
an Angel.]

VOCAL: SACRED CHORAL--WOMEN'S VOICES, ACCOMPANIED

ADM 72 WW1. Christmas Lullaby. Words by Frances McCollin (2')

SSA, Pno. acc./T. Presser, © 1937./Score 5p./Dedicated to Roma Angel.

ADM 71 WW2. Come Hither, Ye Faithful. Christmas Carol--anthem for three-part women's
voices with soprano solo. Tr. by E. Caswall from Adeste fideles (3')

SSA, S. solo, Pno. acc./Oliver Ditson Co., © 1927, 1936./Score 7p./Transcribed by the composer from the original for mixed voices (6 part)./First perf.: Graduate Nurse Glee Club,
Philadelphia, Pa., Dec. 30, 1937.

ADM 71 WW3. A Christmas Carol. In the Bleak Midwinter. See: In the Bleak Midwinter.

ADM 71 WW3. In the Bleak Midwinter. A Christmas Carol. Four-part women's chorus with
piano accompaniment. Words by Christina G. Rossetti (1830-1894)

SSA/Ms./Score 12p./Leslie Marles the transcriber./On cover page pen name "Gabriel," "Noel"
used./Dedicated to Frances Snyder and Lincoln High School Girls' Vocal Ensemble./First perf.:
Symphony Society of Frankford and Abraham Lincoln High School Choir, Philadelphia, Pa.,
June 2, 1960.

ADM 71 WW-4. Mary Sat at Even. Words: Old carol (4')

SSA, Pno. acc./J. Fischer & Bros., © 1931./Score 9p./Dedicated to The Matinee Musical Club
Chorus, Philadelphia, Harry A. Sykes, conductor./First perf.: Matinee Musical Club,
Philadelphia, Pa., Dec. 15, 1931.

VOCAL: SECULAR CHORAL--WOMEN'S VOICES, A CAPPELLA

ADM 72 LUS-1. Motto for Philadelphia Music Club--"Music." Trio for women's voices. Words
     by M. G. Brainard (1837-1905)

SSA/Ms./Score 1p./Date of completion: Feb. 1912.

VOCAL: SECULAR CHORAL--WOMEN'S VOICES, ACCOMPANIED

†ADM 73 LASS-1. Christmas Bells. Words by H. W. Longfellow (3')

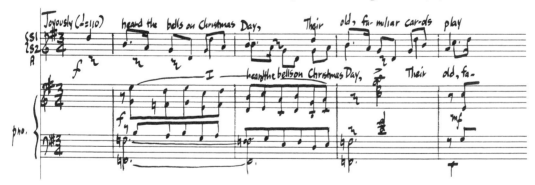

SSA with Pno. acc./Mills Music, © 1947./Score 8p./Prize: Pennsylvania Federation of Music
Clubs, 1947.

*†ADM 73 LASS-2.   The Coming of June.   Words by Margaret Brand   (4')

SSA, Pno. acc./Clayton F. Summy Co., © 1944./Score 9p./Dedicated to Dr. H. Alexander Matthews./Prize: Ginn and Champion, Boston, 1936./First perf.: Philadelphia Music Club, Philadelphia, Pa., Nov. 15, 1944.

ADM 73 LASS-3.   Echoes of the Valley.   Words by Bertha L. P. Butting

SI, SII with Pno. acc./Ms./Score 12p./Date of completion: Mar. 21, 1945.

ADM 73 LASS-4.   The Fly and the Flea.   Words: anonymous

SA with Pno. acc./C. C. Birchard & Co., © 1932./Score 2p./Dedicated to the Westchester Junior Music Festival and its conductor, Victor L. F. Rebmann./First perf.: Junior Chorus of the Westchester Festival, Westchester, Pa., May 12, 1933.

*ADM 73 LASS-6. God's Miracle of May. Words by Frank Dempster Sherman

SSA, Pno. acc./The Arthur P. Schmidt Co., © 1919./Score 6p./First perf.: Manuscript Music
Society Chorus, Philadelphia, Pa., Nov. 25, 1919.

*†ADM 73 LASS-7. Go Not, Happy Day. Words by Alfred Tennyson

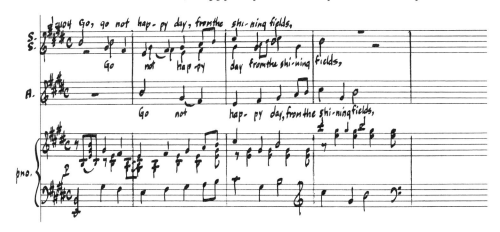

SSA with Pno. acc./J. Fischer & Bro., © 1940./Score 11p./Dedicated to Edith Foster./Prize:
The Eurydice Chorus, 1939/First perf.: Matinee Musical Chorus, Philadelphia, Pa.,
Feb. 4, 1941.

ADM 73 LASS-5. Grasshopper Green. Words by Mildred Harrington (2')

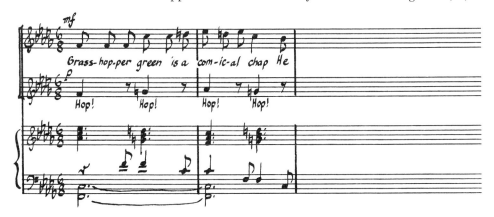

SA with Pno. acc./H. T. FitzSimons Co., © 1945./Score 6p./Dedicated to the Review Club of
Oaklane, Ellen Todd, chorus director.

ADM 73 LASS-8. In the Hammock. Words by Annie Willis McCullough (3')

S.A. with Pno. acc./C. C. Birchard & Co., © 1949./Score 8p./Dedicated to the Crescendo Club of Philadelphia, Mrs. James A. Aikens, director.

*†ADM 73 LASS-9. It Was a Lover and His Lass. Words by William Shakespeare (3')

SAA with Pno. acc./Oliver Ditson Co., © 1952./Score 10p./Dedicated to the Class of June 1951, Philadelphia High School for Girls, Marguerite M. Gill, director./Prize: National Federation of Music Clubs, 1951./First perf.: Philadelphia Chamber Chorus, Philadelphia, Pa., May 9, 1969.

ADM 73 LASS-10. My Garden. Words by Eric Parker (3')

S.A. with Piano acc./C. C. Birchard & Co., © 1936./Score 9p./Dedicated to Alice Frances Arnett./First perf.: Crescendo Club, Philadelphia, Pa., 1948-49 season.

ADM 74 LASS-11.   My Sweet Sally.   Words by Bertha L. P. Nutting   (3')

SI, SII, Pno. acc./Ms./Score 8p./Composed: Mar. 3, 1945-Mar. 12, 1945.

ADM 74 LASS-13.   Now Is the Month of Maying.   Words: anonymous   (4')

S.S.A., Pno. acc./The Arthur P. Schmidt Co., © 1934./Score 10p./Dedicated to Gena Branscombe./First perf.: Philadelphia High School Girl's Chorus, Philadelphia, Pa., June 25, 1934.

ADM 74 LASS-14.   Oh!   Where Do Fairies Hide Their Heads?   Words by Thomas Haynes Bayley
   (1797-1839)   (6')

SI SII AI AII, Pno. acc./The Arthur P. Schmidt Co., © 1927./Score 20p./Dedicated to the
Women's Club Chorus of Easton, Pa., Helen Arny Mecan, conductor.

ADM 74 LASS-15.   O Robin, Little Robin.   Words: anonymous (3')

SSA, Pno. acc./The Arthur P. Schmidt Co., © 1919./Score 4p./First perf.: Philadelphia Music
Club Chorus, Philadelphia, Pa., Jan. 27, 1920.

ADM 74 LASS-16.   Queen Anne's Lace.   Words by May Leslie Newton (3')

SA, Pno. acc./C. C. Birchard & Co., © 1940./Score 4p./Dedicated to Hayden M. Morgan./First
perf.: Crescendo Club, Philadelphia, Pa., 1948-49 season.

*ADM 74 LASS-17.   Snow Flakes.   Words by Mary Mapes Dodge (3')

The Arthur P. Schmidt Co., © 1919./Score 6p./Dedicated to Helen Pulaski Jones, director, and
the Members of the Matinee Musical Club Chorus of Philadelphia./First perf.: Matinee Musical
Club Chorus, Philadelphia, Pa., Jan. 20. 1920.

*†ADM 74 LASS-18.   Spring in Heaven.   Words by Louise Driscoll   (5')

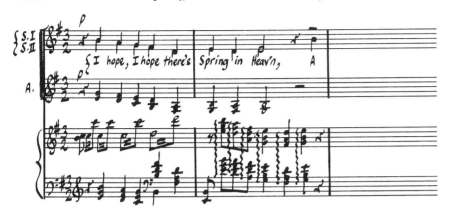

SSA, Pno. acc./The Macmillan Co., © 1931./Score 17p./Dedicated to the Philadelphia Music Club Chorus, Dr. H. Alexander Matthews, conductor./Prize: National Federation of Music Clubs, San Francisco, Calif., June 20, 1931.

ADM 74 LASS-18.   Whispering Dreams.   Words by Bertha L. P. Nutting

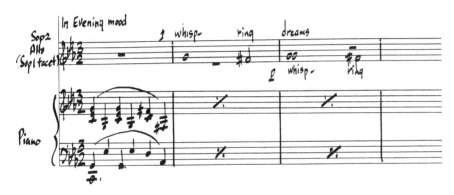

SSA, Pno./Ms./Score 16p.

VOCAL: SECULAR CHORAL, CANTATA--WOMEN'S VOICES, ACCOMPANIED

ADM 75 LAS-1.   Going up to London.   Cantata for women's voices with flute obbligato and piano accompaniment.   Words by Nancy Byrd Turner   (10')

SSA, Fl. and Pno. acc./Carl Fischer, © 1935./Score 24p./Dedicated to the Tuesday Musical Choral Club of Pittsburgh./Charles N. Boyd, conductor./First perf.:   Massachusetts Federation of Women's Clubs Choral Society, Boston, Mass., Jan. 18, 1936.

ADM 75 LAS-2. June. Words by James Russell Lowell (7')

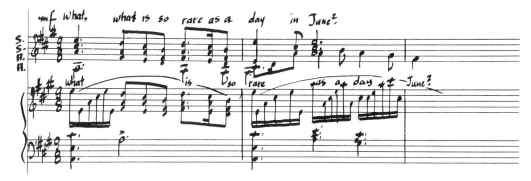

SSAA, Pno. acc./The Arthur Schmidt Co., © 1922./Score 24p./Dedicated to the Orange Musical Art Society, Dr. Arthur Woodruff, conductor./First perf.: Treble Clef Chorus, Haddon Heights, N.J., June 3, 1930.

*†ADM 75 LAS 4. The Singing Leaves. A cantata for women's voices with soprano, tenor, and baritone solos. Words by James Russell Lowell (20')

SSA, SI, Bar. Solos, Pno. acc./Oliver Ditson Co. (Theodore Presser Distributors), © 1918./ Score 28p./Prize: Matinee Musical Club, Philadelphia, 1918./First perf.: Matinee Musical Club, Philadelphia, Pa., Dec. 3, 1918.

*ADM 75 LAS-5. The Sleeping Beauty. Cantata for women's voices. Words by Alfred Tennyson (17')

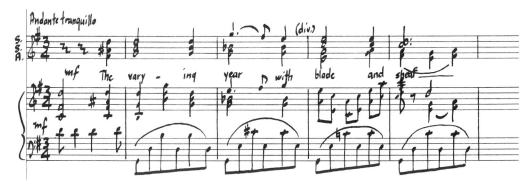

S SA Pno. Acc./Oliver Ditson Co., © 1917./Score 28p./Dedicated to Frances McCollin's parents./ First perf.: Eurydice Chorus, Philadelphia, Pa., Mar. 1, 1918.

ADM 75 LAS-3. 'Twas the Night Before Christmas (A Visit from St. Nicholas). Words by Clement C. Moore

SA, Pno. acc./The Arthur Schmidt Co., © 1923./Score 28p./Dedicated to Edmund McCollin Arnett./Listed as Christmas Cantata for juvenile voices./First perf.: New Century Club Chorus, Philadelphia, Pa., Dec. 1925.

VOCAL: SECULAR CHORAL--MALE VOICES, A CAPPELLA

ADM 76 MC-1. The Ahkoond of Swat. An ode. Male chorus a cappella. Words by George T. Lanigan

TTBB/Ms./Score 22p.

ADM 75 MC-2. The Optimistic Frog. Words by unknown American author

TTBB/Ms./Score 10p./Composed: Apr. 28, 1949, to June 10, 1949./Dedicated to the Germantown Male Chorus, Louis C. Deak, conductor.

VOCAL: SECULAR CHORAL--MALE VOICES, ACCOMPANIED

ADM 77 MA-1. The Four Winds. Chorus for male voices with piano accompaniment. Words by
  Charles H. Luders (5')

TTBB, Pno. acc./H. W. Gray Co., © 1922./Score 19p./Dedicated to The Orpheus Club of
Philadelphia. Dr. Arthur D. Woodruff, conductor, in commemoration of the fiftieth anniversary of the club, 1872-1922./First perf.: Chicago Mendelssohn Club, Chicago, Ill., Feb. 19,
1922.

ADM 77 MA-2. Hunting Song. Words by Sir Walter Scott (5')

The Arthur P. Schmidt Co., © 1923./Score 12p./Dedicated to Dr. H. Alexander Matthews, conductor of the University of Pennsylvania Glee Club./First perf.: Williams College Musical Club,
Philadelphia, Pa., Dec. 18, 1926.

ADM 77 MA-3. Persian Serenade. Chorus setting. Words by Bayard Taylor

TTBB, Pno. acc./Ms./Score 5p./Pen name Garrett Colyn used.

ADM 77 MA-4. A Vagabond Song. Words by Bliss Carman (6')

TTBB, Pno. acc./The Arthur P. Schmidt Co., © 1926./Score 6p./First perf.: Germantown Male Chorus, Germantown, Pa., March 31, 1941.

ADM 77 MA-5. When Earth's Last Picture Is Painted. Words by Rudyard Kipling

TTB, Pno. acc./Ms./Score 18p.

APPENDIX A

List of Frances McCollin's Works That Received National Awards

1916   Anthem, "O Sing unto the Lord"
Manuscript Music Society of Philadelphia

1918   Cantata, Women's Voices, "The Singing Leaves"
Matinee Musical Club of Philadelphia

1918   Anthem, "The Lord Is King"
American Guild of Organists, Clemson Award

1918   Song, "The Winds of God"
Society of Arts and Letters, Philadelphia

1918   Madrigal, "The Nights O' Spring"
Chicago Madrigal Club, W.W. Kimball Co. Prize

1919   Organ Solo, "Caprice" (missing manuscript)
National Federation of Music Clubs, Honorable Mention

1919   Song, "The Midnight Sea"
National Federation of Music Clubs

1921   Anthem (a cappella), "Then Shall the Righteous Shine"
Mendelssohn Club of Philadelphia

1923   Madrigal, "What Care I?"
Chicago Madrigal Club, W.W. Kimball Co.

1925   Anthem (a cappella), "Now the Day Is Over"
Strawbridge and Clothier Radio Competition, Philadelphia

1926   Anthem (a cappella), "Come Hither, Ye Faithful"
Dayton Westminister Choir

1931   Women's Chorus, "Spring in Heaven"
National Federation of Music Clubs

1936   Women's Chorus, "The Coming of June"
Ginn and Company, Boston

1938   Women's Chorus (a cappella)
Sigma Alpha Iota, "The Shepherds Had an Angel"

1939   Women's Chorus, "Go Not Happy Day," Eurydice Chorus,
Philadelphia

147

1941   Anthem (a cappella), "Peace I Leave with You"
       Capital University, Columbus, Ohio

1947   Women's Chorus, "Christmas Bells"
       National Federation of Music Clubs, Pennsylvania Contest

1947   Anthem, "O Little Town of Bethlehem"
       Harvey Gaul Contest

1951   Women's Chorus, "It Was a Lover and His Lass"
       National Federation of Music Clubs, Philadelphia Contest

In addition to these awards given for specific works, Frances McCollin also received general recognition for her overall contribution to music. She was included in the 1940-1941 edition of Who's Who in the East, and in 1951 she received the "Distinguished Daughter of Pennsylvania" award from the Distinguished Daughters of Pennsylvania.

APPENDIX B

Frances McCollin's Membership in Organizations

American Composers' Alliance	Honorary Member
American Guild of Organists	Member
American Society of Composers, Authors, and Publishers	1942
Central Committee for Conscientious Objectors	Member
Distinguished Daughters of Pennsylvania	1951
The Fellowship of Reconciliation	Member
Friedlander Union	Member
Matinee Musical Club	Honorary Member
National Association of American Composers and Conductors	Professional Member
National Federation of Music Clubs	Life Member
New Century Club	Honorary Member
Philadelphia Art Alliance	Artist Member
Philadelphia Music Club	Charter Member
Philadelphia Music Teachers Association	Honorary Member
Women's International League for Peace and Freedom	Member

APPENDIX C

Sponsoring Organizations of Adult and Children's Presentations by Frances McCollin, 1924-1944

Bethlehem Bach Festival

Bryn Mawr Women's Club

Ethical Culture Society

Germantown Women's Club

Indianapolis Symphony Women's Club

Junior League in Baltimore

Junior League in Philadelphia

Main Line School of Music

Matinee Musical Club

Mothers in Council of Germantown

New Century Club

Pennsylvania Federation of Women's Clubs Biennial Convention

People's Symphony Orchestra of Boston, Massachusetts

Philadelphia Art Alliance

Philadelphia Music Club

Philomusian Club

Women's City Club

All Saints' School

Booth Day Camp

Friends' Select School

Friends' Central Day Camp

Germantown Friends' School

Chestnut Hill Friends' Meeting Sunday School

Mignon School

Miss Zain's School

Torresdale School

Valley Meeting Sunday School

APPENDIX D

Works of Frances McCollin Presented on Radio and Film

Medium	Composition/Performers	Year
Station WIP	"Thou Art unto a Flower," Mr. Norris, soloist	1922
Station WJZ (N.Y.)	"O Robin, Little Robin"	1925

Station WCAU, <u>Music in Wartime</u> <u>& in Peacetime</u>	Specific compositions not indicated	1934
Station WFIL	<u>Chorale Preludes</u>, Indianapolis Symphony, Fabien Sevitzky, conductor	1939
Station AMCST (Indiana)	"Christmas Poem," Indianapolis Symphony Orchestra, Fabien Sevitzky, conductor	1940
Station WFIL	"Prelude in A minor," "Prelude in D flat," "Sarabande," "Mother Goose Toccata," Letitia Radcliffe Harris, soloist	1948
Station WOR	"Now's the Month of Maying," Gena Branscombe, conductor	1948
Station WFIL	"Adagio for String Orchestra," WFIL's String Ensemble, Norman Black, conductor	1948
Station KYN	"I Wonder as I Wander" (premiere), Harry Banks, Girard College, organ	1948
Film, <u>Philadelphia: The Growth</u> <u>of an Idea</u>, Divisions of Fine & Industrial Arts of the Philadelphia Board of Public Education	"Adagio," "Heavenly Children at Play," Barozzi String Quartet; "Prelude in A flat minor," Elisabeth Gittlen, pianist; "Nursery Rhyme Suite," Louis Wersen, conductor, Elisabeth Gittlen, pianist	1949
CBS Network	<u>Chorale Prelude</u>, Philadelphia Orchestra, E. Ormandy, conductor	1951
Station WFLN	"Adagio," Indianapolis Symphony, F. Sevitzky, conductor; "Sarabande," Jeanne Behrend, pianist; "Prelude in A major," "Prelude in A minor," Elisabeth Gittlen, pianist; "Mother Goose Toccata," "Ring Out Wild Bells," Temple University Music Dept., Elaine Brown, conductor	1951
Station WTVZ	"Mother Goose Toccata," Zelda Kilgore, pianist	1951
CBS Network	"All Glory, Laud, and Honor," E. Power Biggs, organist	1952
Station WRCV, <u>Christmas</u> <u>Program</u> Sponsored by the Musical Fund Society	Specific compositions not indicated	1963
Station WFLN, <u>Music of</u> <u>America</u>	Specific compositions not indicated	1975
Station WGBH (Boston, Mass.), <u>Morning Pro Musical</u>	"Prelude in D-flat," Anya Laurence, Pianist	1979
Station WRCV	"I Wonder as I Wander," McCurdy Orchestra, Paul White, conductor	n.d.

FRANCES McCOLLIN'S MEMORABILIA

All the primary source materials used have been donated by the McCollin family to the Free Library of Philadelphia and housed in the music department. I have categorized the memorabilia into folders and have created an arbitrary numerical classification for reference. I have annotated the entries by item number with a brief description of the contents of the folders. Reference to these items is made in chapters of the book in the endnotes corresponding to each chapter.

ITEM 1. Alice Graham McCollin.
Information about Mrs. McCollin is contained in this folder. It includes a bank book from the Philadelphia Savings Fund Society in trust for Frances; music with Mrs. McCollin and the original Women's Committee of the Philadelphia Orchestra pictures on the cover; Alice McCollin's obituary printed in several newspapers; copy of her will; West Laurel Hill Cemetery Memorials and the deed to the cemetery land.

ITEM 2. Biographical File of Frances McCollin.
This folder contains interesting biographical material on McCollin, including her poetry and literary creations. Also contained in the folder are Christmas cards created by her. Included is her resume (one prepared as an obituary), an interview (Philadelphia Inquirer Magazine, 25 September 1949); follow-up sheet from the Pennsylvania Institution for the Instruction of the Blind. The essay done for English class by Dorothy Myer, "Frances McCollin, Pacifist Musician," describes the composer physically, talks about her father's influence in her musical background, and her interest in imaginary words, colors, birds, religion, and pacifism. Another essay with no title was written by McCollin herself describing her early musical education.

ITEM 3. Compositions by Friends of Frances McCollin.
This folder contains musical works dedicated to Frances McCollin by John Franco, S. Margerite Maitland, Elisabeth Gest, and Albert Dooner.

ITEM 4. Correspondence of Frances McCollin.
The following sets of letters to Frances McCollin are separated by decades.
    4A   Letters: Dates not given.
    4B   Letters: 1910-1920.
    4C   Letters: 1921-1930.
    4D   Letters: 1931-1940.
    4E   Letters: 1941-1950.
    4F   Letters: 1951-1960.
    4G   Letters: After 1960.

ITEM 5. Correspondence on Particular Musical Compositions.
Several works rated much correspondence, enough to be put in separate folders other than publishers' folders.
    5A   "Hunting Song"
    5B   "Ring Out, Wild Bells"
    5C   "Sleep Holy Babe"
    5D   "A Song of Spring"
    5E   Suite in F

5F	"The Things of Everyday Are All So Sweet"
5G	"The Vagabond Song"
5H	<u>Variation on an Original Theme for Piano and Orchestra</u>
5I	"Welcome Happy Morning"
5J	"What Care I?"
5K	"When Earth's Last Picture Was Painted"

ITEM 6.   Correspondence with Churches: 1983.
The following churches answered letters requesting records of live performances of Frances McCollin's works:
Ness, Earl (First Baptist Church). Letter to author, June 1983.
Ciucci, Anthony (St. Peter's Church). Letter to author, June 1983.
Todd, Reverend Galbraith (Arch Street Presbyterian Church). Letter to author, 14 June 1983.
Henderson, Richard C. (St. Clement's Church). Letter to author, 15 June 1983.
Platt, Fred (St. Paul's Church). Telephone conversation with author, 16 June 1983.
Abbott, Jane (Church of New Jerusalem). Telephone conversation with author, 15 June 1983.
Kerr, Reverend Norman (The Church of the Holy Trinity). Letter to author, 16 June 1983.
Smart, Robert (The Church of the Holy Trinity). Letter to author, 17 June 1983.
Day, Wesley (St. Mark's Church). Letter to author, 20 June 1983.
Gilmore, Gil (Calvary United Methodist Church). Letter to author, 20 June 1983.
Scott, Reverend John (St. Mary's Church, Hamilton Village). Letter to author, 20 June 1983.
Jerome, Mrs. W.D. (St. Luke's Epiphany). Telephone conversation with author, 16 June 1983.
Boggs, Mrs. (Holy Apostle and the Mediator Church). Telephone conversation with author, 17 June 1983.

ITEM 7.   Death of Frances McCollin.
This folder includes Frances McCollin's death certificate, obituary notice, office of the register of wills, copy of will, Letters Testamentary, funeral arrangements, and official receipt of Transfer Inheritance and Estate Tax.

ITEM 8.   Edward McCollin.
Items included in this folder are a biography of the man in the "Record of the Class of 1878, University of Pennsylvania"; genealogy of the McCollin Garrett Family done by George Scattergood; and a Musical Fund program featuring the 1979 Edward McCollin Memorial Fund prize winner.

ITEM 9.   Framed Memorabilia.
One of the framed items is the Philadelphia Orchestra Program of 3, 4, 6 November 1933 with Leopold Stokowski conducting Frances McCollin's "Adagio." The other is her ASCAP membership dated 24 September 1942.

ITEM 10.   Guest Book for 2128 Delancey Place.
Entries begin in 1924 with poems, notes, and signatures of people who dined with the McCollins, such as Elisabeth Gest, Fabien Sevitzky, Frances Wister, Agnes Quinlin, Vladimir Sokoloff, Alexander McCurdy, Orlando Cole, and Leopold Stokowski.

ITEM 11.   Interviews (Taped).
The following interviews were taped live and are in the files.
11A	Andrews, Alice. Interview with author. Philadelphia.
11B	Arnett, Mrs. John. Interview with author. Philadelphia, 9 November 1979.
11C	Arnett, John. Interview with author. Philadelphia, 31 May 1979.
11D	Arnett, Ned. Interview with author. Philadelphia, 16 May 1981.
11E	Behrend, Jeanne. Interview with author. Philadelphia, 19 April 1980.
11F	Marles, Leslie, Interview with author. Philadelphia, 10 June 1981.

ITEM 12.   Interviews (Transcribed).
             This folder includes the written transcriptions of the following interviews also on
             tape, with Mrs. John Arnett, Mr. W. Hillard Comstock, Mr. Leslie Marles, and a
             letter from Eugene Ormandy, refusing an interview.

ITEM 13.   "Just Me." Autobiography by Frances McCollin.
             In 1951 Frances McCollin wrote an autobiography up to the age of thirteen in six
             chapters for the "I Personally Award" of a magazine (whose name is not mentioned
             anywhere), calling it "Just Me." It was left in the hands of Katherine McCollin
             Arnett but some of the pages are missing as well as the final chapter. The chap-
             ter headings are as follows: "Earliest Impressions," "Life Began at Five," "Edu-
             cation," "Detour," "The Curtain Rises," "Finale" (missing).

ITEM 14.   Katherine McCollin Compositions.
             Katherine McCollin, Frances's sister, wrote songs under the name Frank Shepherd-
             son, which are in this folder.

ITEM 15.   Medals.
             In a box there is a medal from the American Guild of Organists, Society of Arts
             and Letters dated 1918, and a medal from the Distinguished Daughters of Penn-
             sylvania dated 1951.

ITEM 16.   Membership in Clubs.
             A list of clubs to which Frances McCollin belonged and a pamphlet on the Fried-
             lander Union.

ITEM 17.   Musical Compositions. Lists.
             The following lists are contained in this folder compiled by Frances McCollin's fam-
             ily:
             Compositions for School Orchestra, Chamber Music, and school orchestra--giving
                 duration, publisher, and location of score during the composer's lifetime.
             Catalogue of compositions by Frances McCollin printed by her family with a photo-
                 graph and resume of McCollin; List of published works and the publishers.
             List of published compositions compiled by Katherine Arnett.
             List of manuscript compositions given to the Free Library by Katherine Arnett.
             Music returned to the library by Katherine Arnett.
             Selected list of compositions for symphony orchestra, chorus and orchestra, school
                 orchestra, string orchestra, and chamber groups.
             Advertisements of various published works and commercial recording by Morning-
                 side Choir.
             Royalty Statement from publications--1950.
             "Five Orchestral Works by Frances McCollin, Distinguished American Composer,"
                 a pamphlet edited and compiled by Wendell R. Martin from program notes for
                 her two chorale preludes, "Adagio" and "Scherzo," and "A Christmas Poem."
             "Directory of American Women Composers with Selected Music for Senior and Junior
                 Clubs" (1976), compiled and edited by Julia Smith.
             Poems--"Where do the Fairies Hide Their Heads" and "Persian Serenade"--used as
                 texts by Frances McCollin.
             List of Orchestral Performances.
             List of performances of Christmas compositions during December 1940.
             List of performances of "Now, All the Woods Are Sleeping" and "All Glory, Laud,
                 and Honor."
             Radio Station WFLN 95.7: Evening of 26 October 1951--a written transcription
                 of what was aired.

ITEM 18.   "Notes made by Edward Garrett McCollin on musical interests and activities of his
             eldest daughter Frances McCollin born at 927 Clinton Street, Philadelphia, Octo-
             ber 24, 1892."
             In a diary-like form, it is a 12-page description of Frances McCollin's early musical
             education (1894-1898) observed by her father, written in 1898. The original is
             hand-written; three copies are included.

ITEM 19.   Performances (Taped).
            The following performances were taped live:
    19A   McCollin, Frances. "I Wonder as I Wander." McCurdy Orchestra, Paul White,
            conductor. Dubbing from McCurdy Broadcast [reel tape].
    19B   McCollin, Frances. Music of Frances McCollin with commentary, under the direc-
            tion of Annette DiMedio. Quintette in F, "May Day," "Going to the Zoo," "Spring,"
            "Canzonetta," "All Glory, Laud, and Honor," "The Things of Every Day," "At
            Eventide," "O Robin, Little Robin," "Sarabande," "Maypole Dance." Recorded by
            Robert Sellman, 19 May 1981 [cassette].
    19C   McCollin, Frances. Quintette in F major for Piano and Strings [no information
            given, reel tape].
    19D   McCollin, Frances. "Overture." Orchestra Society of Philadelphia, Robert Fitz-
            patrick, conductor, 1 April 1979 [cassette].

ITEM 20.   Pictures.
            A folder of autographed pictures of David Bisphani, Emma Nevada, Michael H. Ciofo,
            and Frances McCollin.

ITEM 21.   Pictures (Oversized).
            Pictures of Leopold Stokowski, Fabien Sevitzky, and Eugene Ormandy, autographed.

ITEM 22.   Prizes.
            Prize award lists, Who's Who in the East, material on the Distinguished Daughters
            Award of 1951, and notifications of various awards are contained in this folder.

ITEM 23.   Programs.
            The following programs and announcements of performances are not contained in
            Frances McCollin's scrapbook but found loose in her files. They have been filed
            according to decade:
    23A   Programs: dates not given.
    23B   Programs: 1910-1920
    23C   Programs: 1921-1930
    23D   Programs: 1931-1940
    23E   Programs: 1941-1950
    23F   Programs: 1951-1960
    23G   Programs: After 1960.

ITEM 24.   Publishers/Organizations Correspondence.
            With submitting compositions and settling publications, copyrights, royalties, much
            correspondence was done with each publishing company and organizations like
            ASCAP. The following folders are categorized by published company or organi-
            zation:
    24A   Abington Press.
    24B   ASCAP
    24C   C.C. Birchard Company.
    24D   Boosey and Hawkes.
    24E   Copyright Renewals.
    24F   Ditson.
    24G   Elkan-Vogel
    24H   Flammer Company.
    24I   Fischer.
    24J   FitzSimons.
    24K   Ginn and Co.
    24L   Gray Galaxy.
    24M   Hinds, Hayden, and Eldredge.
    24N   Lawson Gould.
    24O   Mills Music.
    24P   Mitchell and Co.
    24Q   Theodore Presser Co.
    24R   Riccordi.
    24S   Saint Mary's Press.

24T   G. Schirmer.
24U   Schmidt.
24V   Shawnee Press.
24W   WPA Listings.
24X   James White.

ITEM 25.   <u>Recordings.</u>
           The following are private and commercial recordings done of Frances McCollin's
           works. The private recordings play at 78 rpm. The commercial recordings (noted
           as such) play at 33 rpm.
25A   McCollin, F. "All Glory, Laud, and Honor." Indianapolis Symphony, Fabien
           Sevitzky, conductor. Audiodisc.
25B   McCollin, F. "Berceuse for Barbara," 16 November 1947. F. McCollin, pianist.
           Recorded disc.
25C   McCollin, F. "A Christmas Poem" (two sides). Indianapolis Symphony Orchestra,
           Fabian [sic] Koussevitsky. DUBB. Reco-Art Sound Recording.
25D   McCollin, F. "Christmas Fantasia" and musical analysis by composer (two sides).
           Audiodisc.
25E   McCollin, F. "A Christmas Poem" (four sides). Audiodisc.
25F   McCollin, F. "Fantasia on 'O Little Town of Bethlehem.'" The William and Mary
           Choir. PR4 M6478.
25G   McCollin, Frances. "Fantasia" on text of "O Little Town of Bethlehem." Bellefield
           Church Choir. Georgeheid Productions.
25H   McCollin, F. The Festival Chorus (two sides). Temple University, "WRII 640 on
           your dial," 8 November 1951.
25I   McCollin, Frances. "How Living Are The Dead" (two sides). Edna Phillips, harp-
           ist; Robert Elmore, organist. Reco-Art Sound Recording.
25J   McCollin, F., "I Walked with You." Robinson Recording Laboratories. Electrical
           transcriptions.
25K   McCollin, Frances, "I Wonder as I Wander." Harry Banks, organist. Reco-Art
           Sound Recording Company, 18 April 1948.
25L   McCollin, F., "I Wonder as I Wander." McCurdy Orchestra, Paul White, conductor.
           National Broadcasting Company WRCV Recording.
25M   McCollin, F., "The Lord Is My Shepherd" (two sides). Hilda Finley, vocalist;
           Catherine Stockquart accompanist. Reco-Art Sound Recording.
25N   McCollin, Frances. The McCollin Society presents the recorded works of Frances
           McCollin: "Mother Goose Toccata no. 4" from <u>Nursery Rhyme Suite</u> and "Prelude
           in A Minor." Elisabeth Gittlin, pianist. MS-100.
25O   McCollin, Frances, "My Peace I Leave with You" (two sides). Fort Meade Choral
           Society. Reco-Art Sound Recording.
25P   McCollin, F., "Now All the Woods Are Sleeping." Indianapolis Symphony, Fabien
           Sevitzky, conductor. Audiodisc.
25Q   McCollin, Frances. <u>Nursery Rhyme Suite</u> (1st Movement). Illustrated talk on
           "Fantasia." WPEN Symphony Orchestra, Louis Werson, conductor. Robinson Re-
           cording Laboratories. Electrical Transcription. Recorded 27 April 1946.
25R   McCollin, F. "Prelude." Letitia Radcliffe Harris, pianist. WFIL Transcription
           9027A. 9 July 1947.
25S   McCollin, Frances. "Prelude in D Flat for Piano." Elisabeth Gest, pianist. Audio-
           disc.
25T   McCollin, Frances. A Program of Choral Music by Frances McCollin. Morningside
           Choir. RCA E4-QL-2081.
25U   McCollin, F. "Scherzo" (two sides). Indianapolis Symphony, Fabien Sevitzky,
           conductor. Recorded by Division of Visual Education School District of Philadel-
           phia, 13 December 1939.
25V   McCollin, Frances. "Sing Alleluia." West Chester State Teacher's College a Cap-
           pella Chorus, Arthur Jones, conductor. Robinson Recording Laboratories. Elec-
           trical transcription. Recorded 15 December 1944.
25W   McCollin, F., "Sleep Holy Babe" (two sides). Halhe Nowland, vocalist. Reco-
           Art Sound Recording Co., 21 December 1947.
25X   McCollin, F. <u>String Quartette</u> (3rd and 4th Movements). Audiodisc.
25Y   McCollin, F. "Song at Midnight." Robinson Recording Laboratories. Electrical
           transcription.

25Z McCollin, Frances, "Spring in Heaven" (two sides). Octavo Club of Norristown, Marion Spangler, conductor. Reco-Art Sound Recording Company.

25WW McCollin, F., "Suburban Sketches," "Symphonic Poem for Orchestra," and musical analysis by composer (two sides). Robinson Recording Laboratories. Electrical Transcription, 14 July 1944.

25XX McCollin, Frances: Suite in F ("Sarabande") and "Prelude in A-Flat Major." Elisabeth Gittlin, pianist. Audiodisc.

25YY McCollin, Frances, "Tune for Tina" and "Dance for Derek." Presto, 16 November 1947.

25ZZ McCollin, F. "Ye Watchers and Ye Holy Ones." Playback Soundcraft.

ITEM 26. Royalty Accounts.
These accounts are McCollin's statements of earnings from compositions published by Ditson, A. Schmidt, G. Schirmer, C. C. Birchard, Riccordi, T. Presser, J. Fischer, C. Fischer, Galaxy Mills, H.T. FitzSimons, and H.W. Gray from 1918 to 1949.

ITEM 27. Scrapbooks.
Seven scrapbooks were compiled by Frances McCollin's family in chronological order. Each scrapbook is 10 inches by 12 inches with her name and dates engraved on most of the covers of the books of 160 pages. The scrapbooks contain reviews of concerts and works, advertisements of published works and talks, correspondence, and programs. The newspaper articles are very neatly pasted in the book with a family member supplying the name of the newspaper and the date but no page number, a problem when using the articles in footnotes and the bibliography.

27A Frances McCollin. Volume I, Scrapbook.
27B _____. Volume II, 1920.
27C _____. Volume III, 1922, 1923, 1924, 1925.
27D _____. Volume IV, 1926, 1927, 1928.
27E _____. Volume V, 1929, 1930, 1931.
27F _____. Volume VI, 1932, 1933, 1934.
27G _____. Volume VII, 1935, 1936, 1937.

ITEM 28. Short Stories and Memoirs of Frances McCollin by Alice Andrews.
Alice Andrews recalls incidents in her life that involved her aunt, Frances McCollin. The names of the stories are: "The Fallen Bride," "The Gold Cup," "Gaga and Uncle Fabien" [sic], "The Three Marys." The memoirs are events that Alice remembers.

ITEM 29. Stokowski Essays and Letters.
A copy of the petition to keep Stokowski as conductor of the Philadelphia Orchestra, letters defending his position to Frances McCollin, and an essay by her in his defense.

ITEM 30. Stokowski Newspaper Articles.
Newspaper clippings that Frances McCollin and her family saved during the time when Stokowski was conductor of the Philadelphia Orchestra.

ITEM 31. Talks.
This folder contains information about various talks given for adults and children. It includes a resume of Frances McCollin's accomplishments used as publicity for the talks; invitations to the Philadelphia Orchestra talks; advertisements for Talks for Young People and Philadelphia Orchestra talks dated from 1933 to 1946; quotations from the Baltimore Sun and Ithaca, New York Music Club's Magazine.

ITEM 32. Works: Catalogue.
This gray metal box contains a record of the works that are catalogued. On each card is an orange dot that gives the folder number and number of the composition in the files according to the catalogue (chapter 5 of the present volume).

PRINTED SOURCES

Books

Amer, Christine. Unsung. Westport, CT: Greenwood Press, 1980.

THE ASCAP Biographical Dictionary of Composers, Authors, and Publishers. New York: Thomas Y. Crowell, 1966.

Barnes, Edwin. American Women in Creative Music: Tuning in on American Music. Washington, D.C.: Music Educational Publications, 1936.

Block, Adrienne F., and Carol Neuls-Bates. Women in Music: Bibliography of Music and Literature. Westport, CT: Greenwood Press, 1979.

Burt, Nathaniel. The Perennial Philadelphians. Boston: Little, Brown, 1936.

Campbell, Jane. Old Philadelphia Music. Philadelphia: City History Society, 1926.

Chase, Gilbert. America's Music. New York: McGraw-Hill, 1955.

Daniels, Oliver. Stokowski: A Counterpoint of View. New York: Dodd, Mead, 1982.

Dennison, Sam, et al., The Edwin A. Fleisher Music Collection of Orchestral Music in the Free Library of Philadelphia, Boston: Hall, 1979.

Dictionary of American Biography. 1963 ed. s.v. "McCollin, Frances."

Ellinwood, Leonard. The History of American Church Music. New York: Morehouse-Gorham, 1953.

Elson, Louis C. The History of American Music. New York: Macmillan, 1915.

Elson, Arthur, and Truette Elson. Women's Work in Music. Boston: L.C. Page, 1931.

Farrell, Gabriel. The Story of Blindness. Cambridge, MA: Harvard University Press, 1956.

Fleisher, Edwin A. The Edwin A. Fleisher Music Collection in the Free Library of Philadelphia. 2 vols. Philadelphia: Privately printed, 1933 (vol. 1); 1945 (vol. 2).

Gerson, Robert A. Music in Philadelphia. Philadelphia: T. Presser, 1940.

Hixon, Don L., and Don Hennessee. Women in Music: A Biobibliography. Metuchen, NJ: Scarecrow Press, 1975.

Howard, John Tasker. Our American Music. New York: Thomas Y. Crowell, 1965.

Howard, J.T., and A. Mendel. Our Contemporary Composers. New York: Thomas Y. Crowell, 1941. Reprinted by Ayer (Salem, NH) 1975.

Hughes, Rupert. Contemporary American Composers. Boston: L.C. Page, 1900.

Ireland, Norma. Index to Women of the World from Ancient to Modern Times. Westwood, MA: F.W. Faxon, 1970. Distributed by Scarecrow Press.

Keller, Helen. The World I Live In. New York: Century, 1908.

Kupferberg, Herbert. Those Fabulous Philadelphians: The Life and Times of a Great Orchestra. New York: C. Scribner's Sons, 1969.

Lukacs, John. Philadelphia Patricians and Philistines, 1900-1950. New York: Farrar, Straus, Giroux, 1981.

National Cyclopedia of American Biography. Vol. 43, 1961. ed. s. v. "McCollin, Frances."

Pennsylvania Federation of Music Clubs. Music and Musicians of Pennsylvania, Gertrude Rohrer, compiler. Port Washington, NY: Kennikat Press, 1940.

Pool, Jeannie. Women in Music History: A Research Guide. New York: Jeannie Pool, 1977.

Reis, Claire. Composers in America. New York: International Society for Contemporary Music, 1932.

Schalk, Carl, ed. Key Words in Church Music. St. Louis: Concordia, 1978.

Schleifer, Martha Furman. "William Wallace Gilchrist: Life and Works." Ph.D. diss., Bryn Mawr College, 1976.

Smith, Julia. Directory of American Women Composers, with Selected Music for Senior and Junior Clubs. Chicago: National Federation of Music Clubs, 1970.

Smith, William James, ed. Granger's Index to Poetry. New York: Columbia University Press, 1973.

Spaeth, Sigmund, ed. Music and Dance in Pennsylvania, New Jersey, and Delaware. New York: Bureau of Musical Research, 1954.

Stern, Susan. Women Composers: A Handbook. Metuchen, NJ: Scarecrow Press, 1978.

Two Centuries of American Musical Composition: The Etude Music Magazine, Souvenir of the Sesqui-Centennial, 1776-1926. Philadelphia: Presser, 1926.

Upton, George. Woman in Music. Boston: J.R. Osgood, 1880.

Upton, William Treat. Art Song in America. Boston: Oliver Ditson, 1930.

Wienandt, Elwyn A., and Robert H. Young. The Anthem in England and America. New York: Free Press, 1970.

Wister, Frances Anne. Twenty-five Years of the Philadelphia Orchestra. Philadelphia: Edward Stern, 1925.

Newspapers and Other Periodicals

Newspapers are listed in alphabetical order; articles under each newspaper title are listed in chronological order.

"America's Women Composers: Up from the Footnotes." Music Educators Journal 65/5 (January 1979): 28-41.

"Frances McCollin." Musical America 51/9 (10 May, 1931): 52-55.

"Frances McCollin Interview." Diapason (January 1934): 12.

New York Times. "Miss McCollin, Composer, Dies." 17 February 1960, p. 19.

Philadelphia Evening Bulletin. "Review." 10 August 1932, p. 11B.

Philadelphia Inquirer. "Alice McCollin Dies." 20 October 1958, p. 20.

_____. "Frances McCollin." 25 September 1944, p. 14.

_____. Martin, Linton. "Jazz Jolts Effect of Classic Music--Traditions Are Shattered When Hearer Calls Out Demand for Repetition." 10 January 1929. Included in McCollin Scrapbook, p. 27.

_____. Martin, Linton. "Review." 4 November 1933, p. 14.

Philadelphia Public Ledger. "Frances McCollin." 16 March 1913. Included in McCollin scrapbook I, p. 21.

_____. "A New First for Philadelphia and a Girl!" 13 March 1918. Included in McCollin scrapbook I, p. 62.

_____. Philadelphia Orchestra: Stokowski conducts Program with New Works by Local Composer. 4 November 1933. Included in McCollin scrapbook, p. 7.

"Points and Counterpoints." New Music Review (January 1934): 40-41.

Tick, Judith. "Women as Professional Musicians in the United States, 1870-1900." Yearbook for Inter-American Musical Research (1973): 93-133.

Zeisler, Fanny Bloomfield. "Women in Music." American Art Journal 58 (17 October 1891): 1-3.

NAME INDEX

TITLE INDEX